Moselle River Trail

From Metz to the Rhine

An original *bikeline*-guide

VERLAG**ESTERBAUER**

bikeline®-guide Moselle River Trail
© 2004-2013, **Verlag Esterbauer GmbH**
A-3751 Rodingersdorf, Hauptstr. 31
Tel.: +43/2983/28982-0, Fax: -500
E-Mail: bikeline@esterbauer.com
www.esterbauer.com
3rd Edition, Summer 2013
ISBN: 978-3-85000-473-2

Please quote edition and ISBN number
in all correspondence!

We wish to extend our thanks to all the people whose hard work helped make this book possible, and especially to the many readers who have sent us corrections and information to keep the book as up to date as possible.
The bikeline-Team: Heidi Authried, Beatrix Bauer, Markus Belz, Michael Bernhard, Michael Binder, Veronika Bock, Petra Bruckmüller, Sandra Eisner, Roland Esterbauer, Gabi Glasstetter, Dagmar Güldenpfennig, Tobias Klein, Martina Kreindl, Bettina Müllauer, Eveline Müllauer, Gregor Münch, Karin Neichsner, Niki Nowak, Carmen Paradeiser, Julia Pelikan, Christian Schlechte, Erik Schmidt, Martina Specht, Matthias Thal, Martin Trippmacher, Martin Wischin, Wolfgang Zangerl.

Cover photos: Cochem: Tourist-Information Ferienland Cochem; Fähre: Saar-Obermosel-Touristik e.V.; Bernkastel-Kues: Carmen Dusi;
Photo credits: Birgit Albrecht: 25, 84, 106, 110, 113, 124; Carmen Dusi: 70, 86; Gemeinde Perl: 33, 50; Gemeinde Perl, L. Weiler: 32, 51; Gemeinde Trittenheim, Otmar Britz: 65; Heidi Authried: 26, 53, 68, 82, 84, 90, 92, 96, 119, 120, 121, 125; Koblenz-Touristik: 132; Koblenz-Touristik©P!ELmedia: 133; Mairie de Metz, Christian Legay, Marc Royer: 18; Mosellandtouristik: 7; Office National du Tourisme Luxembourgeois: 36, 37; Saar-Obermosel-Touristik: 54, 57; Stefan Decker: 91, 92, 121, 122; Tbias Klein: 7, 21, 22, 24, 27, 28, 30; Tourist Info Ferienland Cochem: 124, 126; Tourist-Information Ferienland Cochem, Christoph Gerhartz: 98; Tourist-Information Ferienland Treis-Karden, Julia Görres: 128; Tourist-Information Römische Weinstrasse: 62, 64, 78; Tourist-Information Traben-Trarbach: 88; Tourist-Information Treis-Karden: 102, 104; Tourist Information Trier: 40. 42, 44, 46, 47, 73; Treis-Karden: 126; Verkehrsamtes Ruwer: 75, 76; Verkehrsamt Neumagen-Dhron: 66; Wolfgang Zangerl: 16, 22, 32

Cartography created with *axpand*
(www.axes-systems.com)

GPS-Track Download
The GPS tracks for this book is available after registration on the internet:
www.esterbauer.com
Productcode: 473-88Gh-A6fm

365eumb082es/mismib

bikeline

What is bikeline?

We are a team of writers, cartographers, geographers and other staff united by our enthusiasm for bicycling and touring. Our project first "got rolling" in 1987, when a group of Vienna cyclists came together to begin producing bicycling maps. Today we are a highly successful publisher that offers a wide range of bikeline® and cycline® books in five languages covering many European countries.

We need your help to keep our books up-to-date. Please write to us if you find errors or changes. We would also be grateful for experiences and impressions from your own cycling tours.

We look forward to your letters and emails (redaktion@esterbauer.com),

Your bikeline team

Preface

The vineyard-lined Moselle River valley provides a uniquely inviting setting for an especially enjoyable bicycle tour. Trace some 310 kilometers of the river's meandering bends and curves while learning about its rich and varied history. Test whether the light and fruity Moselle wines live up to their reputation, and stroll (or roll) through the ancient narrow lanes and splendid avenues of the river's charming villages and historic cities.

This cycling guide includes detailed maps of the countryside and of many cities and towns, precise route descriptions, information about historic and cultural sites as well as background information and a comprehensive list of overnight accommodation. The one thing this guide cannot provide is fine cycling weather, but we hope you encounter nothing but sunshine and gentle tailwinds.

3

map legend

Cycle route

Main cycle route, low motor traffic

———— paved road
– – – unpaved road
······· bad surface

Cycle path / main cycle route, without motor traffic

———— paved road
– – – unpaved road
······· bad surface

Excursion or alternative route, low motor traffic

———— paved road
– – – unpaved road
······· bad surface

Excursion or alternative route, without motor traffic / cycle path

———— paved road
– – – unpaved road
······· bad surface

———— other cycle routes
ooooooo planned cycle path
xxxxxxx closed cycle path
⚓ooooo ferry connection

Vehicular traffic

▪▪▪▪▪▪ cycle route with moderate motor traffic

▪▪▪▪▪▪ cycle route with heavy motor traffic

▪▪▪▪▪▪ cycle lane

———— road with moderate motor traffic

———— road with heavy motor traffic

Gradient / distance

➤ steep gradient, uphill
➤ light to moderate gradient
╲ 3,2 ╱ distance in km

············· cobbled street
———— tunnel
5424 UTM-grid (2km)
⇨ cycle route direction
▢ city map
5 waypoint

Cycling informations

🔧 bike workshop*
🚲 bike rental*
🚲 covered bike stands*
🚲 lockable bike stands*
▲ dangerous section
▲ read text carefully
🪜 stairs*
)(narrow pass, bottleneck*

In city maps

P parking lot*
P garage*
✉ post office*
A pharmacy*
H hospital*
F fire-brigade*
U police*
🎭 theatre*

* selection

Scale 1 : 50.000

1 cm ≙ 500 m   1 km ≙ 2 cm

| 0 | 1 | 2 | 3 | 4 | 5 | 6 | 7 | 8 | 9 | 10 km |

Important or worth seeing thematic informations

Schönern	picturesque town
(i▲⊖)	facilities available
🏨	hotel, guesthouse
🏠	youth hostel
⚑	camping site
△	simple tent site*
i	tourist information
🗐	shopping facilities*
♈	kiosk*
🍽	restaurant
🍴	resting place*
⌂	covered stand*
⌣	swimming pool
⌣	indoor swimming pool
♂♀	church, monastery
🏰	palace, castle
♂	ruins
🏛	museum
✺	excavation
✳	other place of interest
🐾	zoo
⚑	nature reserve, monument
☀	panoramic view

Topographische Informationen

♂	church
♀	chapel
♁	monastery
♂	castle
♂	ruins
♀	tower
♀	TV/radio tower
♂	power station
⚡	transformer
♂♂	windmill
✳	windturbine
†	wayside cross
⌐	cave
✕	mine
♀	lighthouse
⊂⊃	sports field
☗	monument
✈	airport, airfield
⛴	boat landing
♀	natural spring
⊟	waste water treatment plant
⊖	international border
	country border
	district border

	forest
	rock, cliff
	marshy ground; heath
	vineyard
	cemetary
	garden
	commercial area
	quarry, open cast mining
	glacier
	dunes, beach
	shallows
	embankment, dyke
	dam, groyne
	motorway, expressway
	main road
	secondary main road
	minor road
	carriageway
	track
	road planned/under construction
	railway with station
	narrow gage railway

5

Contents

City maps

The Moselle River Trail

The Moselle River offers everything one could expect from a typical European wine-growing region. Countless orderly rows of grapevines cover much of the steep slopes that rise from both sides of the river. Nestled among the many vineyards lie timeless quaint villages and hamlets. Charming old stone or half-timbered houses meet the eye in every direction. Many of these buildings are used to press, store and serve the delicious white wines that the region's mild climate helps produce. As the region's inhabitants like to say, "There's always time for a glass of wine."

And at the end of the day, find restful accommodation in an old half-timbered farmhouse snuggly set between the vineyards.

As if the idyllic verdant landscape were not enough, the river is lined with imposing castles and the ruins of old fortifications, each of which has its own story to tell. Learn the strange tales and legends that have become part of the valley's long and colourful history.

That history does not, of course, begin with the Romans. But it is they who left many of the oldest and most impressive edifices. Their splendid palaces, amphitheaters, public baths, bridges, aqueducts and many other structures bear witness to the knowledge and skill they brought to this corner of central Europe. After the arrival of Christianity, it was the Frankish kings and the Archbishops of Trier that ruled the land, and built many of the castles, churches, cloisters and monasteries that today recall the Moselle's long and rich history.

About the cycling route

Length

The Moselle river trail from Metz to Koblenz covers about **310 kilometres**. Additionally there are a further 125 kilometres of alternative routes and excursions.

Road surface and traffic

The quality of the route is excellent. Sections that are unpaved or difficult to negotiate are rare. The route mostly follows paved bicycle paths and street. Longer unpaved sections are only to be found between Bullay and Seheim as well as between Cochem-Cond and Treis-Karden, where the route runs through a nature reserve.

Traffic volume along the Moselle is varied. The route mostly follows bicycle paths, quiet streets and bicycle lanes. Sections along busy roads are rare. If you find the traffic adjacent to a bicycle lane or path too high, you usually have the option of changing to a quieter route on the other river bank using one of the many bridges and fwerries along the way.

In the introductory text at the beginning of each section you will find an indication as to which side of the river the main route follows. In the route description tips emphasise where we suggest you change to the other river bank.

Signage

The bicycle route along the Moselle river is signposted all the way between Metz and Koblenz. From the Saar-Moselle confluence by Konz to the end of the route in Koblenz you follow the signage for the D5 route, although this is not always complete. The detours and excursions described in this guide are not always signposted.

Cycling in Germany

The popularity of bicycle tourism and mountain biking in Germany has grown significantly in the last fifteen years. Recognizing this trend, German tourism agencies have helped support the creation of many bicycle trails, networks and long-distance routes. These follow separate designated bikeways or quiet minor and secondary roads. Only rarely do marked bicycle routes make use of busy roads. Most cities also feature extensive networks of bicycle trails and routes that help make bicycle riding safe and pleasant. In general, riding a bicycle in Germany is relatively safe – partly because there are many well-designed bikeways and routes, partly because motorized traffic is accustomed to sharing the roads with an ever-growing number of cyclists.

RentaBike Miselerland

This is the name of a special bicycle rental organisation in Luxembourg. This system operates through numerous local rental operators in the Moselle region by Luxembourg, whereby the bicycles don't have to be returned to the same place, but can be left with any of the members in the region. These are identified in our guide with the note "RentaBike, see page 8".

For further information ✆ 00352/621217808 or under www.rentabike-miselerland.lu

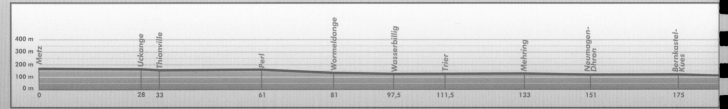

Planning your tour

Important Telephone numbers

International telephone codes:
Germany: 0049
France: 0033
Luxembourg: 00352
When calling internationally, dial the international country code followed by the local area code without the initial "0". Please note that in France the local area code must also be dialled when calling within the local area.

Central Information Offices

German National Tourist Board (GNTB), Beethovenstr. 69, D-60325 Frankfurt/Main, ☎ 069/974640, www.germany.travel

Moselle Tourisme, 2-4 rue du Pont Moreau, F-57000 Metz, ☎ 0033/387/375780, www.tourismus-moselland.com

Office Régional de Tourisme Région Moselle Luxembourgeoise, 115, route du Vin, L-5416 Ehnen, ☎ 00352/26747874, www.region-moselle.lu

Mosellandtouristik, Kordelweg 1, D-54470 Bernkastel-Kues, ☎ 06531/9733-0, www.mosellandtouristik.de
www.moselland-radtouren.de

Saar-Obermosel-Touristik e.V., Granastr. 22, D-54329 Konz, ☎ 06501/60180-40, Fax: -424, www.saar-obermosel.de

Touristinfo Sonnige Untermosel, Bahnhofstr. 44, D-56330 Kobern-Gondorf, ☎ 02607/4927, Fax: 4958,

www.sonnige-untermosel.de

Rheinland-Pfalz Tourismus, Löhrstraße 103-105, D-56068 Koblenz, ☎ 0261/91520-0, Fax: -40, www.rlp-info.de

Deutsch-Luxemburgische Tourist-Information, Moselstr. 1, D-54308 Langsur-Wasserbilligerbrück, ☎ 06501/602666, Fax: 605984, www.lux-trier.info

Arrival & Departure

Arrival & departure by air

Visitors from countries beyond Europe can reach Germany or France easily with commercial airlines. The international airport at Frankfurt/Main is, after London's Heathrow, the second-largest airport in Europe and offers excellent connections to international routes. Once you have arrived in Europe, trains and buses offer excellent alternatives to air travel, particularly as there are no direct connections between Metz-Nancy-Lothringen airport and larger international airports other than Paris.

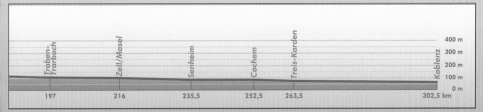

Traben-Trarbach	Zell/Mosel	Senheim	Cochem	Treis-Karden		Koblenz
197	216	235,5	252,5	263,5		302,5 km

400 m / 300 m / 200 m / 100 m / 0 m

Arrival & departure by rail

Due to the constantly changing prices and conditions for transport of a bicycle by rail we suggest that you inform yourself about your personal rail travel at the following addresses.

German Rail (DB): ☎ 01805/996633 (€ 0.14/Min. from landline, mobile telephone prices differ), Mon-Sun 8-20, Information about train connections and bicycle transport (Key selection: 15 or code: Fahrrad), Prices, booking and reservations, www.bahn.de, www.bahn.de/bahnundbike

Automatic DB time table information:
☎ 0800/1507090 (free from landline),
☎ 0180/5221100 (from mobile telephone, subject to charge)

ADFC, German Cycling Federation.: Further information under; www.adfc.de/bahn

French Rail (SNCF):
National: ☎ 3635 (€ 0.34/min),
International: ☎ 0033/892353535,
www.sncf.com/en

Luxembourg Rail (CFL): For timetable information ☎ 00352/(0)2489/2489, further information and booking; www.cfl.lu

Bicycle Transport

Hermes-Privat-Service:
☎ 0900/1311211 (€ 0.60/Min.)
www.privatpaketservice.de
For information and online booking klick on the link "Koffer/Fahrradversand."

Arrival and departure by car

The starting point Metz is easily reached by car, as it lies directly on the A 4. The return trip from Koblenz with a bicycle, however, takes more than 6 hours and requires one to change trains several times. We therefore do not recommend arriving by car.

Bike & rail

Because a train line does not run along the entire length of the Moselle, it is not always possible to board a train for some part of the trip. The following stretches and towns are connected by rail: Along the Moselle between Metz and Trier. Downstream from Trier the railway line leaves the river and it is not until between TrabenTrarbach and Bullay and then again between Cochem and Koblenz that the railway line follows the river.

In Germany, bicycles can be brought onto any trains that are marked with a bicycle symbol in the schedule, provided the passenger holds a bicycle ticket and there is space available in the designated bicycle compartment. Advance reservations are recommended, and are required at least one day in advance on most long-distance trains that accept bicycles.

In France:

Bicycles can be transported on almost all regional (TER) and some 'intercités' trains in specially designated spaces free of charge. Space is limited and you cannot book, so arrive early. Bicycles are accepted only on long-distance trains and some 'intercités' trains that are marked with a bicycle symbol in the train schedule. The bicycle must be loaded by the passenger; some trains require a space to be booked and a fee ma apply. When you reach the train station from which you wish to depart, look for a bicycle compartment. Bicycle transport on trains crossing the border between France and Germany usually only possible as hand luggage. Bicycles can be taken as hand luggage on all trains if transported in a cycle bag measuring no more than 120 x 90cm.

Bike & Ship

Numerous passenger ships ply the Moselle between April and October. Most towns have a dock where ships can stop, but because these are so numerous, they are not shown in this book. Information about passenger ships is included in the information section for the more important towns and cities along the Moselle.

For exact information about arrival and departure times, check the schedules posted by operators at docks where their ships stop. A complete and current schedule for passenger ships on the Moselle and Saar rivers can be ordered at no cost from Mosellandtouristik (see page 9).

Please note that the locks along the river are serviced in mid June every year, which restricts shipping for a couple of days.

Bike & Bus

A bus service known as the **RegioRadler Moseltal (Linie 333)** operates three time daily between Trier and Bullay along the Moselle, over the towns Ruwer, Schweich, Neumagen, Bernkastel-Kues and Traben. The bus takes up to 22 bicycles.

For further information:

Verkehrsverbund Region Trier (VRT), Bahnhofspl. 1, D-54292 Trier, ☎ 01805/131619 (€ 0.14/Min. from German landline, mobile telephones up to € 0.42/Min.), www.regio-radler.de Reservations recommended!

Moselbahn (Region Mosel), Moselbahnstr. 7, D-54470 Bernkastel-Andel, ☎ 06531/9680-10, Fax: 9680-50, www.moselbahn.de

Bicycle Taxi

The Koblenz company Aktiv-Taxi takes up to eight bicycles in a special bicycle trailer. Further information: **Aktiv-Taxi**, Hermannstr. 15g, D-56076 Koblenz, ☎ 0261/9737537, www.aktiv-taxi.de.

Accommodation

Because the Moselle valley is a popular tourist destination, it offers an extensive selection of guest rooms and hotels at every price and comfort level. Even with the large number of beds available, during the busy vacation and grape harvest seasons, making reservations in advance is recommended.

Bicycle tours with children

The Moselle bike trail is also suitable for children as it is generally flat and at least one bank of the river offers quiet bicycle paths away from the traffic. Due to the numerous bridges and ferries, it is also easy to change from one bank to the other as the need arises.

Seasons

The Moselle region has a special charm at every time of the year. In spring, the valley's many orchards are in bloom. In June the inns and restaurants along the river open their gates to bicycle tourists and other guests.

The valley's main tourist season, however, is in autumn, when the foliage changes colour and local wine growers begin the grape harvest. Many of the small wine-making villages and towns decorate their streets and houses for traditional annual wine festivals.

Another favorite date on the calendar is the "Happy Mosel Day", when the Moselle Valley between Schweich and Cochem (on the left side as far as Winningen), is closed to motorized traffic for a day. For more information see www.mosellandtouristik.de

What to wear

The right choice of clothing is an important factor to consider for a successful cycling tour. The range of outdoor clothing avaible has become very large and somewhat confusing: so here are a few ground rules to optimal cycling wear.

Most important is the "onion principle": where several layers, each fulfilling a specific function, are worn separately or in various combinations.

The first layer should wick sweat away from the body. The next layers, if required; an insulating layer to keep warm and an outer layer to keep wind and rain out, but still be of a breathable fabric.

The best materials are either synthetics (light, low moisture retention) or wool (heavier, but is warm even when wet and does not take on odours). Cotton is not as well suited as it absorbs and retains moisture easily and is slow to dry.

Good quality is especially important by the cycling pants. Comfort is essential.

Bicycle tour operators

If you do not wish to take your bicycle tour independently, there are private operators who can help organize your vacation. These companies can provide bicycles and other equipment, group tours led by experienced guides, hotel reservations and baggage transport, enabling you to plan an entirely unencumbered tour of the river according to your needs.

The German-language tour operators can also provide information, some of which is available in English. Euro-Bike, an operator based in the United States, also runs a bicycle tour along the Moselle.

Euro-Bike, Austin-Lehman Adventures, P.O. Box 81025, Billings, MT 59108-1025 ✆ 1-800-575-1540, info@eurobike.com, www.eurobike.com

Eurobike, Mühlstr. 20, A-5162 Obertrum am See, ✆ 0043/6219/7444, Fax: 8272, eurobike@eurobike.at, www.eurobike.at

Pedalo, Kickendorf 1a, A-4710, Grieskirchen, ✆ 0800/2400999 (free from A & D), otherwise ✆ 0043/7248/635840, info@pedalo.com, www.pedalo.com

Rückenwind Reisen, Am Patentbusch 14, D-26125 Oldenburg, ✆ 0049/441/485970, info@rueckenwind.de, www.rueckenwind.de

Mosellandtouristik, Kordelweg 1, D-54470 Bernkastel-Kues, ✆ 06531/9733-0, www.mosellandtouristik.de www.moselland-radtouren.de

Austria Radreisen, J.-Haydn-Str. 8, A-4780 Schärding, ☎ 0043/7712/55110, Fax: 4811, office@ausria-radreisen.at, www.austria-radreisen.at
Rad & Reisen GmbH, Schickg. 9, A-1220 Wien, ☎ 0043/1/4053873-0, Fax: -17, office@fahrradreisen.at, www.radreisen.at
velociped, Alte Kasseler Str. 43, D-35039 Marburg, ☎ 0049/6421/886890, Fax: 8868911, info@velociped.de, www.velociped.de
Donau-Touristik GmbH, Ledererg. 4-12, A-4010 Linz, ☎ 0732/2080, www.donautouristik.com, E-Mail: office@donautouristik.com
velotours Touristik, E.-Sachs-Str. 1, D-78467 Konstanz, ☎ 0049/7531/98280, Fax: 982898, info@velotours.de, www.velotours.de

About this book

This cycling guide contains all the information you need for your cycling vacation along the Moselle from Metz to Koblenz: Precise maps, a detailed description of the route, a comprehensive list of overnight accommodation, numerous detail maps of cities and towns, and information about the most significant sights. And all that information comes with our **bikeline pledge**: The route described in this book has been tested and evaluated in person by one of our editors! To assure that the book is as up-to-date as possible, we welcome corrections submitted by readers and local officials or businesses. We cannot, however, always check and confirm such changes before deadline.

The maps

The detail maps are produced in a scale of 1:50,000 (1 centimeter = 500 meters). In addition to exactly describing the route, these maps also provide information about roadway

quality (paved or unpaved), climbs (gentle or steep), distances, as well as available cultural and culinary highlights.

Even with the most precise map, consulting the written description of the route may be necessary at times. Locations where the route is difficult to follow are shown by the ⚠ symbol on the maps, the same symbol can then be found in the written description where the route is explained in detail.

Note that the recommended main route is always shown in red or purple; alternative and excursion routes in orange. The individual symbols used in the maps are described in the legend on pages 4 and 5.

Route altitude profile

The route altitude profile in the introduction provides a graphic depiction of elevations along the route, the total length, and the location of larger towns and cities along the way. Additionally, a detailed altitude profile is provided at the beginning of each section which shows many of the smaller centers along the way as well as the waypoints, giving you a direct reference to the maps and route description. The latitude profiles do not show every individual small hill and dip, but only the major changes in elevation. On the detail maps smaller gradients are shown by arrows that point uphill.

The text

The maps are supplemented by a written text that describes the route starting in Metz and proceeding down the Moselle to Koblenz. Key phrases about the route description are indicated with the   symbol.

Many distinctive or important positions along the route are marked as waypoints with consecutive numbers **1**, **2**, **3**, ... and, to help with navigation, are to be found with the same symbol in the maps.

The description of the main route is also interrupted by passages describing alternative and excursion routes. These are printed in orange colour.

Furthermore, the names of important **villages**, towns and cities are printed in bold type. If a location or community has important points of interest, addresses, telephone numbers and opening times are listed under the headline with the name of the place.

Descriptions of the larger towns and cities, as well as historic, cultural and natural landmarks help round out the travel experience. These paragraphs are printed in italics to distinguish them from the route description.

TIP Text printed in purple indicates that you must make a decision about how your tour shall continue. For instance, there may be an alternative route that is not included in the tour description, or a turn-off to another location.

ALTERNATIVE These also indicate excursion suggestions, interesting sights or recreational facilities that are not directly on the main route.

List of overnight accommodation

The last pages of this cycling guide provide a list of convenient hotels and guest houses in virtually every village or town along the route. This list also includes youth hostels and campgrounds.

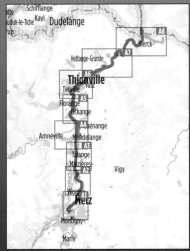

The Moselle River Trail begins in Metz, in the state of Lorraine, north eastern France. The route takes you via the small town of Thionville towards the Schengen tri-state point, where the borders of Germany, France and Luxembourg meet. From this point the Moselle forms the border between Germany and Luxembourg. Before you continue, it is worth making a visit to Schengen, which came to prominence with the Schengen Agreement, or getting involved in excavations of the Roman villa Borg near Perl.

The route in this section is flat and runs almost exclusively along paved surfaces. You follow mostly bicycle paths and quiet streets, with traffic to be expected only on a few short sections. Between Mondelange and Koenigsmacker there is a route along both sides of the river.

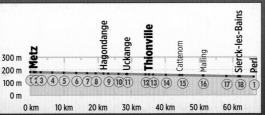

Metz (F)

Postal code: 57000; Area code: 0387

- 🛈 **Office du Tourisme de Metz,** 2, Place d'Armes, ✆ 555376, www.tourisme.metz.fr
- 🛈 **Moselle Tourisme,** 2-4, rue de Pont Moreau, ✆ 375780, www.moselle-tourisme.com
- ⛴ **La Lorraine Fluviale,** Plan d'eau, ✆ 761024, Departs: May-Aug., daily 13:30, 14:45, 16, 17:15, Sept., Wed, Sat, Sun 13:30, 14:45, 16, 17:15. Restaurant ship and river cruises in the Metz area.
- 🏛 **Museum "La Cour d'Or",** 2, rue du Haut Poirier, ✆ 201320, Open: Mon, Wed-Fri 9-17, Sat, Sun 10-17. Includes collections on archaeology, Merovingian jewelry, choral cabinets of St. Pierre aux Nonnains, richly decorated wooden ceilings and painted works from the Metz school.
- 🏛 **Centre Pompidou-Metz,** 1, parvis des Droits de l'Homme, ✆ 153939 Open: Mon, Wed-Fri 11-18, Sat 10-20, Sun 10-18. A modern, contemporary museum with three galleries.
- ⛪ **Cathédrale Saint-Etienne,** built between the 13th and 16th centuries with yellow Jaumont limestone and featuring more than 6,500 m² of windows, including windows designed by Marc Chagall.
- ⛪ **Saint-Maximin** (12.-15 Jh.), Open: 9-17:45. The Romanesque church houses beautiful stained-glass windows by Jean Cocteau.
- ⛪ **Basilica of Saint-Pierre-aux-Nonnains,** Rue de la Citadelle, ✆ 399200, Open: mid June-mid Sept., Tue-Sun 14-19, mid Sept.-mid June, Sat 13-18, Sun 14-18. The 4th c. AD Roman building was later converted to a church and is one of the oldest churches in Europe, the oldest in France.
- 🛈 **Chapelle des Templiers (Templar chapel),** ✆ 399200. The late Romanesque chapel was built between 1180 and 1220.
- ⛪ **Palais du Gouverneur,** 9, rue de la Citadelle. Constructed 1902-1904 in the neo-Renaissance style.
- ✳ **Arsenal,** 3, Avenue Ney, ✆ 399200, Open: Tue-Sat 14-19, Sun 14-18. A military armory built during the reign of Napoleon III. Includes a concert hall with 1,300 seats for performances in all artistic categories.
- ✳ **Porte des Allemands (German gate),** Boulevard Maginot, ✆ 555376. The two, slim round towers of the mighty town gate were already built in 1230. The two larger defensive towers date from 1445.
- 🌳 **Jardin de l'Esplanade**
- 🌳 **Parc de la Seille,** rue Louis Le Débonnaire
- 🏖 **Metz Plage,** Plan d'eau, ✆ 555613
- 🏊 **Piscine olympique,** 44, rue Lothaire, ✆ 682640
- 🚲 **Cycles et Motos Majchzak,** 71, rue des Allemands, ✆ 741314
- 🛵 **Mob d'emploi,** 6/7, place du Général de Gaulle, ✆ 745043

Metz, the capital of Lorraine, is a modern town of more than 300,000 inhabitants. While the industrial development that fueled Metz's growth dominates the cityscape, the old city near the Moselle retains its charm, with historic edifices, numerous gothic churches and baroque public parks.

The history of Metz goes back about 3,000 years ago. Oppidum was the capital of the Celtic Mediomatrics. After the Romans conquered the region, they renamed the city Divodorum Mediomatricorum. Over the centuries, the name became Mediomatrici, then Mettis, which is the source of the present name, Metz. Under the Romans, Metz emerged as the largest Gaulic-Latin centre of the time, more important even than Paris.

The town's large number of churches is a result of the middle ages, when Metz was the seat of a bishopric. As commerce and trade thrived, the people of Metz secured the right to exist

Metz, Cathédrale Saint-Etienne

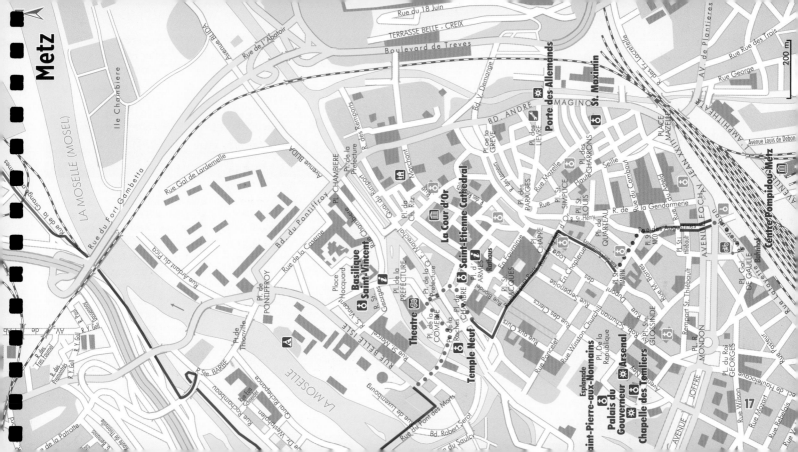

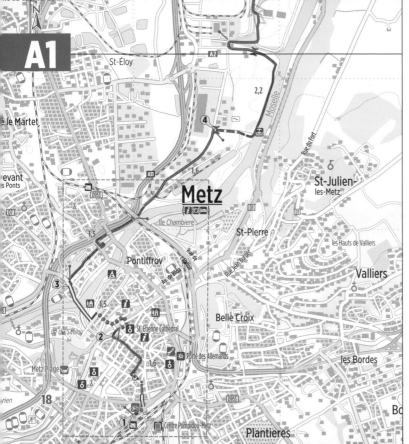

St-Éloy

Metz

St-Julien-
les-Metz

St-Pierre

les Hauts de Valliers

Pontiffroy

Valliers

Belle Croix

St. Etienne Cathedral

les Bordes

Porte des Allemands

Metz Plage

Plantieres

Centre Pompidou-Metz

Metz, la Porte des Allemands

as a free town of the Holy Roman Empire.

The Reformation marked another important part of the town's history. A majority of the population converted to Protestantism, and sought the protection of France. In return, King Henry II of France took control of the bishoprics of Metz, Toul and Verdun. As the strategic value of Metz grew, France heavily fortified the town. Germany occupied the town twice in the last 130 years. American forces liberated Metz in 1944 and returned Lorraine to French control.

Metz to Thionville   34 km

TIP Because a bicycle path has not yet been built out of the centre of Metz and the available options are limited, we have tried to identify the best and fastest route for beginning the Moselle cycle tour. Even so, it is necessary to ride about one kilometer along a major road with heavy traffic.

1 From the train station take the **Rue Vauban** to the right towards the tower ⌇ turn left by the tower into the bicycle path along the **Rue des Augustins** ⌇ cross the busy Avenue Foch ⁓ straight ahead past the square ⁓ where the street bends to the left, continue straight ahead into the bus and bicycle lane ⁓ follow the left bend of the Rue Lasalle ⁓ you ride on cobblestones across a square, at the end of which you turn right into the pedestrian street **Rue de Parmentiers** ⁓ at the end of the street just before the staircase, turn left into the pedestrian street **Rue de la Tête d'Or** ⁓ continue through three intersections, at the last of which you get a first look at the cathedral to the right ⁓ continue straight ⁓ **2** turn right into **Rue du Faisan** ⁓ as you reach a square continue straight ahead along the street ⁓ following the **Place de La Chambre** you pass on the left of the cathdral ⁓ follow the left bend of the street and ride across the bridge ⁓ turn left immediately after the bridge ⁓ turn right in front of the church

⁓ you cross a cobbled bridge ⁓ at the T-intersection turn left and ride along the edge of the park ⁓ turn right into the street **Rue du Pont des Morts** ⁓ you ride over the bridge across the Moselle ⁓ straight after the bridge ⁓ **3** turn right into the street 100 m before the next bridge ⁓ turn left immediately and ride to the bank of the waterway, the **Canal de Metz** ⁓ turn right into the path along the canal.

Charles le Téméraire

The bicycle route between Metz and Apach was named after Charles le Téméraire (Charles the Bold), who was the last duke of the house of Valois-Burgund. Born in 1433, he came to power in 1467 and captured Nancy, the capital of Lothringen in 1475. He was, however, not able to hold his conquests very long and died in 1477 by a battle at the gates of

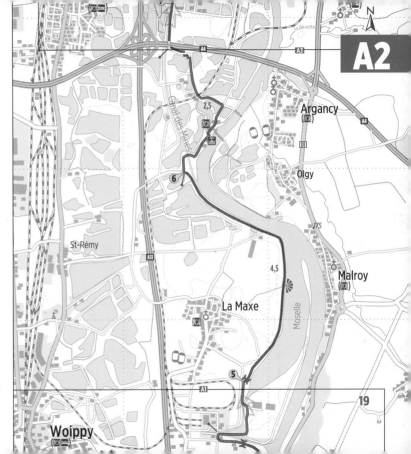

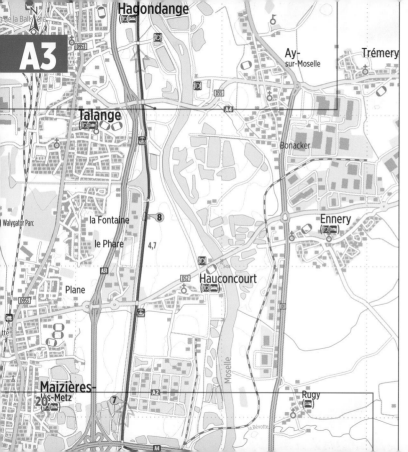

Nancy. His lands were divided after his death, Burgundy going to the kingdom of France and the areas in the north (by Thionville) going to the Habsburgs.

The path takes you along the canal ∼ after passing under the bridge follow the path up onto the bridge and cross the canal ∼ turn right at the end of the bridge ∼ follow the paved bicycle path between the freeway and the canal out to the Moselle ∼ you pass under two bridges, after which the path leaves the river and you must continue to the right along the street **Rue de la Grange aux Dames** ∼ after crossing railway tracks keep left at the fork ∼ you follow the **Rue du Trou aux Serpents** through an industrial area ∼ **4** after 1.25 km turn right into the gravel road opposite the IKEA warehouse ∼ where the gravel road turns to the right, ride straight ahead into the paved bicycle path ∼ the path takes you along the Moselle for a short distance ∼ after a left bend continue straight ahead into the street ∼ at the T-intersection turn right ∼ ride over the first bridge and turn right into the paved lane between the two canals ∼ keep left as you pass under a conveyor bridge ∼ after passing fields turn left across the small bridge ∼ follow the paved lane for a short distance ∼ **5** take the next turnoff to the right past the gate into the bicycle path towards Argancy ∼ you bypass the village of **La Maxe** as you follow the paved path along the river ∼ after passing several ponds the path takes you past a gate and over a little bridge ∼ **6** at the T-intersection turn right towards Thionville ∼ follow the road across a bridge over the canal.

This canal, the **Canal de Fer de la Moselle** *(English: Canal of the Iron*

The canal by Mondelange

Mines of Moselle), was built between 1867 - 1932 to transport metallurgical products from the steel centres between Metz and Thionville and will be your companion for part of the journey to Thionville.

Continue on the paved road as it winds its way past several buildings and a hydroelectric power station ～ the paved road takes you between ponds and under a railway bridge ～ continue straight ahead ～ a bicycle path eventually begins on the left hand side, quickly changing to the right side of the road ～ after passing under the freeway bridge the path continues along the left side of the road once

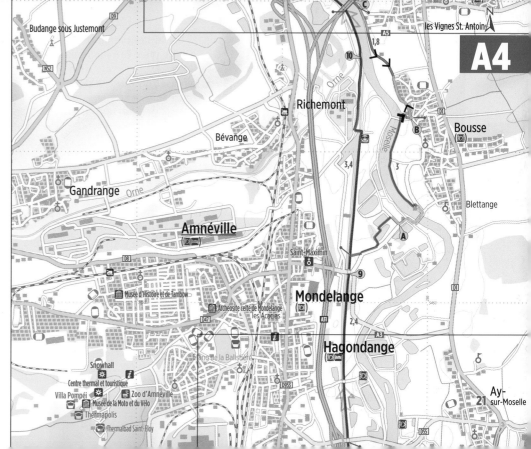

Budange sous Justemont

les Vignes St. Antoine

Richemont

Bévange

Bousse

Blettange

Gandrange

Amnéville

Saint-Maximin

Mondelange

Musée d'Histoire et de Tambow

Archeosite celte de Mondelange
les Acacias

Hagondange

Snowhall

Centre thermal et touristique

Villa Pompéi

Zoo d'Amnéville

Musée de la Moto et du Vélo

Thermapolis

Ay-
sur-Moselle

Thermalbad Saint-Éloy

21

Swan on the canal

more ~ **7** after passing under a conveyor bridge ride to the left onto the bicycle path diretly along the Moselle canal ~ near Hauconcourt you pass under the D 52 road bridge.

EXCURSION Follow the D 52 to the left if you wish to get to Maizières-les-Metz, where you will find Europe's largest roller coaster.

Maizières-lès-Metz (F)
Postal code: 57280; Area code: 0387

- ✱ **Walygator Parc**, Voie Romaine, ✆ 307007. The amusement park boasts over 60 different attractions and is home to Europe's largest roller coaster since 2010 (Duration: 2,28 min., Top speed: 110 km/h).

8 you pass the **Talange locks** before passing under a small bridge ~ as you pass Talange

you pass under the bridge of the D 55 ~ a short distance later you pass under another small bridge.

EXCURSION You can use this quiet bridge or the next road bridge 1.5 km further along for getting to Hagondange, Mondelange and the thermal spa Amnéville on the left side of the canal.

Hagondange (F)
Postal code: 57300; Area code: 0387

- ℹ **Office de Tourisme**, Place Jean Burger, ✆ 703527
- 🏖 **Recreational lake "la Ballastière"**, Espace de la Ballastière, Open: July-Aug., 10-18.

Mondelange (F)
Postal code: 57300; Area code: 0387

- ⛪ **Saint-Maximin** (18th c.)
- 🏛 **Archeosite celte de Mondelange (Celtic excavations museum)**, 6, avenue de l'Europe, ✆ 172606, Open: Mon-Wed 9-12 & 14-17, Thur 9-12, Fri 14-17. Exhibitions from the excavations of a celtic necropolis.

Amnéville (F)
Postal code: 57360; Area code: 0387

- ℹ **Office de Tourisme**, Rue du Bois de Coulange, ✆ 701040
- 🏛 **Musée de la Moto et du Vélo (Motorcycle and bicycle museum)**, Rue du bois de Coulange, ✆ 87723557, Open: Feb.-Oct., Tue, Thur, Fri 13:30-18, Wed, Sat, Sun 10-12 & 13:30-18. Exhibits of motorcycles and bicacles from the 19th and 20th c.

- 🏛 **Musée d'Histoire et de Tambow**, Rue Clémenceau, ✆ 069/9923916. The history museum covers mainly WWII and the Russian prisoner of war camp in Tambow, where mostly French forced servicemen were held.
- ✱ **Centre thermal et touristique Docteur Jean Kiffer d'Amnéville-les-thermes**, ✆ 87701040. The 800 ha area contains numerous tourist attractions: A theme park (✆ 734560), an aquarium (✆ 703661), a golf course (✆ 713013), a 3D cinema (✆ 708989), boating lake, ice rink (✆ 711126), a ropes course (✆ 734560) and much more.
- ✱ **Snowhall**, ✆ 151515. One of the world's longest indoor ski slopes (620 m.)
- 🦒 **Zoo d'Amnéville**, 1, rue du Tigre, ✆ 702560, Open: April-Sept., 9:30-19:30, Oct.-Mar., 10 am to dusk. It is considered one of

On the Moselle by Illange

the most beautiful zoos in Europe and includes a 1 ha Gorilla inclosure, where two Gorilla groups live.

- 🕿 **Thermal spa Saint-Éloy**, Bois de Coulange, ☎ 701909
- 🕿 **Thermapolis**, Avenue de l'Europe, ☎ 718350
- 🕿 **Villa Pompéi**, Avenue de l'Europe, ☎ 709920

Amnéville is one of the five Thermal spas in Lorraine and boast a very large choice of recreational activities.

Continue on the bicycle path beside the canal ∿ **9** you pass under the busy road bridge opposite Mondelange.

ALTERNATIVE 200 m after the bridge there is a turnoff to the right which you can use to get onto the signposted bicycle path along the right bank of the Moselle.

Along the right bank to Thionville   13 km

Follow the signposted turnoff to the right ∿ after a short distance follow the path along the left side of a road ∿ the path takes you away from the road and between ponds ∿ turn right at the T-intersection at the end of the bicycle path ∿ **A** at the next T-intersection turn left and follow the street over the bridge ∿ turn left immediately after the bridge ∿ after 100 m ride onto the paved bicycle path leading away to the left ∿ follow the path along the Moselle towards Bousse ∿ follow the path up to the town.

Bousse (F)

Continue straight ahead along the street ∿ **B** turn left at the T-intersection ∿ immediately left again into the side street **Rue Hector Berlioz** ∿ turn left at the next oppotunity into the side street **Rue Ravel** ∿ in the right bend ride straight ahead into the bicycle path, which takes you between fields back down to the river ∿ continue into the quiet street at the edge of Guénange.

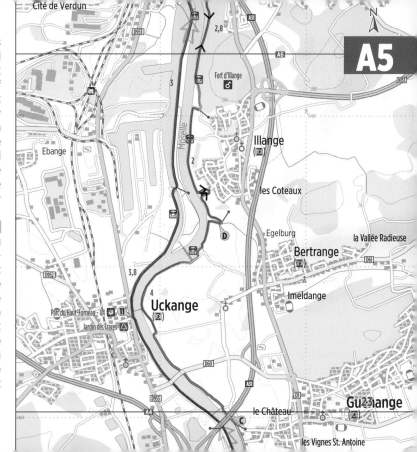

Guénange (F)

Ride along the one-way street beside the river ∼ in the right bend of the street by the last houses ride straight ahead into the bicycle path ∼ **C** you pass below the freeway bridge ∼ keep left at the next T-intersection and follow the paved path along the bank of the Moselle ∼ you pass below another road bridge ∼ Uckange comes into view on the opposite bank, where the heritage listed smelter dominates the riverside skyline ∼ continue on the path beside the river towards wenig Illange ∼ the path ends and you continue straight ahead along the paved road ∼ immediately after passing the **Barrage d'Illange** turn left into the bicycle path along the river ∼ the path takes you in a loop around an inlet and over a small bridge **D** ∼ the path takes you along a field and up to the edge of Illange ∼ at the intersection by the houses keep left on the bicycle path towards Thionville. Going right will take you into Illange.

Illange (F)

🛡 Fort d'Illange. The fortification was erected atop a hill on the east bank of the Moselle after the German empire had taken the Alsace-Lorraine region during the Franco-Prussian War (July 1870 to May 1871). It was part of a complex of 11 fortifications around Thionville and Metz, built to defend against a French attack. The fortification is now an open-air museum.

Continue along the river bank ∼ the path takes you away from the river bank ∼ the path ends by a small bridge ∼ turn right and immediately left into the asphalt road beside the field ∼ you pass a picnic area and continue on the bicycle path along the river bank ∼ **E** you pass under the freeway bridge as you reach the edge of Yutz ∼ turn left into the street by the parking area ∼ after the right bend turn left into the street **Rue des Artisans** ∼ at the T-intersection turn left and ride under the bridge ∼ turn right

Uckange, U4 steel smelter

immediately after the bridge and ride up to the roundabout.

◾**CENTRE** To reach the centre of Thionville turn right at the roundabout to get onto the bridge, which takes you over the canal, the railway and the Moselle into Thionville.

Thionville (F) see page 26

To stay on the main route along the left bank of the Moselle, continue straight ahead along the canal past Mondelange (refer to Map A4) ∼ cross to the left side of the canal at the next bridge ∼ turn right after the bridge and follow the path along the canal past an industrial area **10** you cross the Orne river at its confluence with the Moselle ∼ the bicycle path now takes you along the Moselle and under the freeway bridge ∼ you pass under another road bridge before reaching Uckange.

Uckange (F)

Postal code: 57270; Area code: 0382

✳ **Parc du Haut-Forneau - U4**, 1, rue du Jardin des Traces, ✆ 573737, Open: Apr.-Nov., Tue-Sun 14-18:30, Fri, Sat 20:30-24. The heritage protected smelter is used for guided tours covering the history of mining and metallurgy.

🏛 **Jardin des Traces (Garten of traces)**, 1, rue du Jardin des Traces, ✆ 865596, Open: Apr.-Oct., Tue-Sun 14-18:30, Night visits: Fri,

Sat 20:30-24. The 4 ha industrial wasteland is divided into three subject areas: Alchemy, steel working and energy.

You follow the path along the river bank past Uckange ~ **11** you near the **D 953**, where the U4 steel smelter can be seen to the left ~ continue along the river out of the town ~ the path eventually takes you along the canal once more ~ as you near the large harbour turn right across the bridge over the canal ~ follow the road along the right side of the canal ~ at the end of the canal ride to the left over both bridges by the locks ~ turn right immediately after the second bridge towards Manom ~ follow the path along the river bank and under

Thionville

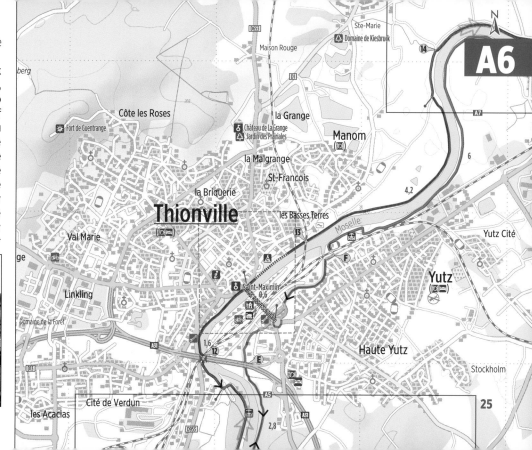

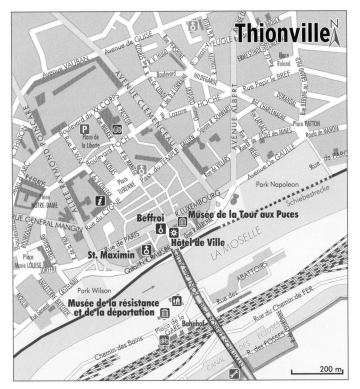

Thionville N

the road and railway bridges **12** ~ continue along the river bank into Thionville.

Thionville (F)

Postal code: 57100; Area code: 0382

- **ℹ️ Office du Tourisme**, 16, rue du Vieux Collège, ✆ 533318, www.thionville.fr
- **🏛 Musée de la Tour aux Puces**, Cour du Château, ✆ 2549 or 822552, Open: Tue-Sun 14-18. Regional museum
- **🏛 Musée de la résistance et de la déportation**, ✆ 556615. Regional museum to the resistance movement and deportation.
- **St. Maximin** (1755-1759), ✆ 533318
- **Beffroi.** The watchtower dates from the 12th c.
- **Hôtel de Ville** (town hall). The former Clarist convent dates from 1629.
- **Fort de Guentrange (Guentrange Fortress)**, Guided tours May-Sept., Sat, Sun 3 pm. Erected around 1900, the fortification was intended to protect Thionville and its important railway hub.
- **Pierron Cycles**, 1, Route de Metz, ✆ 827335
- **Cycles Garsi**, 1, rue des Artisans, ✆ 561076
- **Holiday Bike**, rue Jean Renoir, ✆ 884516
- **Mob d'emploi**, place de la Gare, ✆ 590548

Thionville (German; Diedenhofen) is the thrid largest city in Lorraine and second only to Metz in its importance as an urban centre in the northern Moselle region. The Thionville-Illange harbour just south of the city is the largest river port in France for the transport

Church in Basse-Ham

of metallurgical products and benefits from its ideal connection to river, road and rail transport.

It is the most important port on the Canal des Mines de Fer de la Moselle, linking Metz and Thionville.

Thionville to Perl 31 km

ALTERNATIVE From Thionville you have the choice of continuing your journey on the left or the right bank of the Moselle as far as bis Koenigsmacker.

Right bank to Koenigsmacker 11 km

To reach the left bank route from the right bank, follow the signs towards Gare de Thionville and Yutz up onto the bridge in Thionville ~ you cross the Moselle, the railway and the canal ~ by the roundabout turn left into the street **Rue de Couronné** ~ follow the street straight ahead ~ turn right just before the bridge with the parking bays on both sides ~ follow the bicycle path along the canal ~ at the end of the path follow the signs to the left.

Yutz (F)

F At the T-intersection turn left and ride under the railway underpass ~ follow the bicycle path past the parking area and the playing fields ~ from the tree-lined avenue follow the path to the right past the picnic area ~ turn left across the small bridge towards Basse-Ham ~ soon the cooling towers of the the Cattenom nuclear power plant come into view ~ the path takes you past an industrial area and along the bank of the Moselle ~ you pass under a conveyor bridge ~ **G** after rounding the river bend keep left at the fork to stay on the path along the river.

Haute Ham (F)

The bicycle path takes you to the right up to the road ~ turn left and follow the bicycle path along the road ~ after a short distance the path leaves the road again.

CENTRE To reach the centre of Basse-Ham, continue straight ahead along the road.

Basse-Ham (F)

Ø Saint-Willibord (18. Jh.)

The bicycle path once again follows the river bank ~ you cross the stream **La Bibiche** as

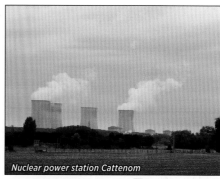

Nuclear power station Cattenom

you bypass Basse-Ham ~ **H** the bicycle path ends by a small boat loading facility and you continue straight ahead on the street ~ a bicycle path begins again after a short distance and you continue along the river ~ at the end of the bicycle path continue straight ahead on the street towards Apach ~ in the left bend of the street turn right into the bicycle path, where you are once again on the main route. To your right lies Koenigsmacker.

To take the main route along the left bank out of Thionville simply continue on the path along the river bank ~ you must dismount and push along the Promenade ~ **13** you pass under a railway bridge as you leave Thionville ~ to your left lies the village of Manom.

Manom (F)

Postal code: 57100; Area code: 0382

6 **Château de La Grange**, Open: Apr.-June, Sept., Oct., Sat, Sun/Hol., Jul., Aug., daily ℓ 538503. The residence dates from the 18th c.

🔺 **Jardin des Prairiales**, ℓ 538503, Open: Jun.-Aug., daily 14-18, Apr., May, Sept., Oct., Sat, Sun/Hol 14-18. The palace gardens were laid out in 2007 according to its predecessor from the 18th c.

🔺 **Domaine de Kiesbruck**, Sainte Marie, ℓ 582389 or 061/6932542. The park is an angler's paradise as its 7 ha of water are reserved for fishing.

Continue along the Moselle ~ the mighty cooling towers of the Cattenom nuclear power plant rise in the distance ahead of you ~ by the small parking bay continue straight ahead along the paved field road ~ **14** keep right just before the small bridge ~ follow the bicycle path along the river bank ~ you pass a transformer station and continue straight

Monument to the allied forces, Cattenom

across the small road ~ back along the river ~ the path ends by a parking area, where you pass a monument to the allied forces ~ keep right by the restaurant and follow the street along the river.

Turn left at the restaurant to reach Cattenom.

Cattenom (F)

Postal code: 57570; Area code: 0382

🛈 **Communauté de Communes de Cattenom et Environs (service tourisme)**, 2, avenue de Gaulle, ℓ 820560

🔖 **Monument to the allied forces**. A monument on the banks of the Moselle recalls the crossing of the river by American forces on 09.11.1944.

The cooling towers of the Cattenom nuclear power plant can be seen from afar. It is the third most powerful in France, producing 8% of the country's electricity in 2007. The plant is controversial, especially in Germany and Luxembourg, due to lacking safety standards. At the end of the street continue straight ahead into the bicycle path ~ **15** cross the

river over the barrage and turn right ~ you follow the paved lane back along the river bank ~ after a left bend you ride along the canal and soon reach a parking area ~ continue straight ahead onto the road, which takes you to the right over the locks ~ in the right bend after crossing the locks turn left into the bicycle path ~ follow the path along the canal ~ at the 3-way intersection turn left over the small bridge.

Turning right at the 3-way intersection will bring you into the centre of Koenigsmacker.

Koenigsmacker (F)

The path passes numerous ponds as you continue along the Moselle ~ you pass under a road bridge as you reach Malling ~ at the end of the bicycle path keep right and follow the street ~ turn right at the T-intersection.

Malling (F)

16 Continue straight ahead at the intersection in the centre of the village ~ turn right towards Gavisse and ride onto the bridge across the Moselle ~ in the left bend turn right into the paved side road ~ immediately left into the

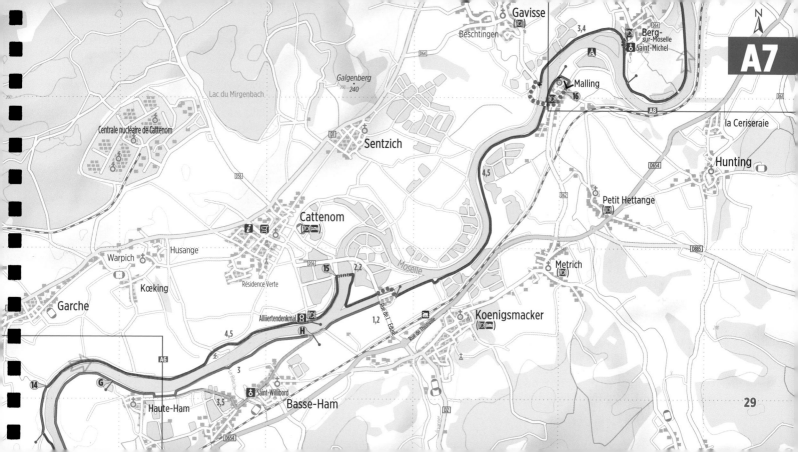

Gavisse
Beschtingen
3,4
Berg-
sur-Moselle
Saint-Michel
Malling
16
la Ceriseraie
Galgenberg
240
Lac du Mirgenbach
D64
D64
Sentzich
Hunting
Centrale nucléaire de Cattenom
D1
4,5
D654
D62
Petit Hettange
D56
D885
Cattenom
Moselle
Metrich
Husange
Warpich
D56
15
2,2
Résidence Verte
Kœking
Koenigsmacker
Garche
Alliiertendenkmal
1,2
Rue de l'Église
Rue de Thionville
4,5
A6
H
3
14
G
3,5
Saint-Willibord
Haute-Ham
Basse-Ham
D2
D654

bicycle path ～ follow the path along the river bank ～ you pass below Berg-sur-Moselle as you ride through a river bend.

Berg-sur-Moselle (F)

⛪ Saint-Michel (1737)

Continue on the path along the river ～ as you near Haute-Kontz you cross a small bridge over the **Gander** ～ **17** turn right at the T-intersection on the **D 64**. From here the river valley narrows and you begin to see vinyards.

Haute-Kontz (F)

⛪ Saint-Hubert (1734)

Just before reaching Contz-les-Bains turn right into the bicycle path along the river.

Contz-les-Bains (F)

⛪ Saint-Jean-Baptiste (1869-1871)

🏛 **Marcel-Levy monument**. The pilot died during the landing of the Allies in the Provence on the 15th of Sept. 1944.

As you leave the village you ride under a road bridge and pass the **Marcel-Levy monument** ～ follow the left bend to the road and turn left ～ ride onto the bridge and cross to the other bank of the Moselle ～ turn left at the end of the bridge towards the camp ground ～ turn left again before the railway tracks

Sierck-les-Bains

～ ride past the **camp ground**. To reach the centre of Sierck-les-Bains, take the second railway underpass ～ the main route continues straight ahead along the river.

Sierck-les-Bains (F)

Postal code: 57480; Area code: 0382

ℹ 🚲 **Office de Tourisme**, 3, place Morbach, ✆ 837414, www.otsierck.com

⛪ **Chapelle de Marienfloss**, ✆ 837414

🏰 **Château des Ducs de Lorraine**, Rue du Château, ✆ 836797, Open: May-Sept., Mon-Sat 10-19, Sun/Hol 10-20, Mar., Apr., Oct., Nov., Mon-Sat 10-16, Sun/Hol 10-17. The palace was once the favourite residence of the dukes of Lorraine. Today one can visit the towers, granary, the powder magazine, the arsenal and the warehouse.

🚲 **Camping de Sierck-les-Bains**, Chemin des Tilleuls, ✆ 837239

You cross the stream **Ruisseau de Montenach** ～ **18** turn right shortly after through the narrow railway underpass ～ turn left onto the street ～ continue straight ahead on the bicycle path ～ parallel to the railway tracks into Apach ～ the bicycle path ends by the railway station just after crossing the stream **Ruisseau de Manderen**.

Apach (F)

Postal code: 57480; Area code: 0382

ℹ **Maison de la Nature (House of Natur)**, 28, rue de l'Europe, ✆ 887749. Information about the Montenach nature reserve, which is well known for its wild orchids.

🏛 **Apach Eiffel Tower**. A 9 m tall replica of the Eiffel Tower in Paris stands on the border between France and Germany.

EXCURSION From the railway station in Apach you can take an excursion to Malbrouck castle. This excusion requires some stamina however, as the castle lies on a hill more than 200 m above the Moselle. The effort is rewarded with a visit to the medieval castle complex and a fanstastic view over the Moselle valley.

Gandren

Schengen
Europäisches Museum

Killebësch

Apacher Eiffelturm

0,5

B407

Oberperl

Schneeberg
430

Hammelsberg
354

Hammelsberg

Naturschutzgebiet Hammelsberg

Deutschland
France

Hirschenberg
425

Merschweiller

1,8

Apach

Belmach

Haute-Kontz

Saint-Jean-Baptiste

Contz-
les-Bains

Saint-Hubert

Moselle

Marcel-Levy-Denkmal

Stromberg
310

Maison de la Nature

Château de Malbrouck

Château de Mensberg

Ruisseau de Manderen

3,5

Kitzing

Mande

4,2

D654

D64

Rettel

D64

18

Rustroff

370

Kirsch

Kasserkopp
355

Château des Ducs de Lorraine

Sierck-
les-Bains

Chapelle de Marienfloss

D654

A7

3,4

D64

Berg-
sur-Moselle

Saint-Michel

D61

D654

Malling

Excursion to the
Château de Malbrouck   13 km

From the railway station turn right into the **Rue de la Gare** ～ cross the main street slightly to the right into the **Rue de l'Eglise** ～ at the end of the street keep right and follow the **Rue de l'Ecole** ～ you pass the school ～ follow the street out of Apach and turn left at the T-intersection ～ keep right at the fork and continue along the paved lane ～ you ride through an undulating landscape of woods and meadows to Kitzing.

Château de Malbrouck

Kitzing (F)

Turn right at the T-intersection in the village and ride over the bridge ～ continue steeply uphill to the **D 64**, where you turn left ～ follow the main road to the next village.

Manderen (F)

You ride uphill into the village ～ in the right bend ride straight ahead into the side street towards Château de Malbrouck ～ keep right at the intersection ～ you cross a small stone bridge and ride uphill ～ in the left bend ride straight ahead towards Château de Malbrouck and follow the small road steeply uphill to the castle.

Château de Malbrouck (F)

♿ Château de Malbrouck, ☎ 0387/350387, Open: Apr., May, Sept.-Dec., Mon 14-17, Tue-Fri 10-17, Sat, Sun/Hol 10-18, June-Aug., Mon 14-18, Tue-Fri 10-18, Sat, Sun/Hol 10-19.

Malbrouck castle, located on the peak of the hill Meinsberg, is visible from afar and lies close to Germany and Luxembourg. Also known as Meinsberg castle, the complex was built between 1419 and 1432. At the end of the 20th c. it was completely renovated, allowing visitors to experience the imposing castle complex in its entirety.

Europe monument in Schengen

To continue along the main route in Apach, ride straight ahead past the railway station ～ keep right at the fork just after the station ～ after a short distance turn left into the bicycle path ～ at the end of the path turn right and ride uphill ～ the Apach Eiffel Tower lies ahead to the right, you must turn left onto the bicycle path before reaching the main road ～ ⊙ you now cross the French-German broder, leaving the Lorraine region and riding into the state of Saarland ～ turn left before the roundabout and follow the bicycle path downhill.

Perl

CONNECTION To reach Schengen and the route along the left bank in Luxemburg ride out to the roundabout and turn left across the bridge over the Moselle.

Schengen (Lux)

Postal code: 5444; Area code: 00352

🛈🏛🚲 **Centre Europeen Schengen**, (Tourist information and museum), Rue Robert Goebbels, ✆ 26665810, Open: Easter-Sept., Tue-Fri 10-18, Sat, Sun/Hol 11-18, Oct.-Easter, Tue-Fri 10-17, Sat, Sun/Hol 11-17. The interactive museum provides information about the Schengen Agreement as well as about the wine village. Also RentaBike, see page 8.

This small wine grower´s village on the Moselle came to promenience through the Schengen Agreement of 1985. This agreement guaran-tees the free movement of people and goods between the signatory states.

To continue into Perl, turn right at the T-intersection and ride under the bridge 〜 turn left at the T-intersection and follow the street Bahnhofstraße 〜 keep left towards the railway station.

Perl

Postal code: 66706; Area code: 06867

🛈 **Tourist information „Schengener Eck"**, Trierer Str. 28, ✆ 66-0, www.perl-mosel.de

✳ **Roman Villa Borg**, about 5 km east of Perl, ✆ 06865/9117-0. Open: Feb.-Mar. & Nov.-Dec., Tue-Sun 11-16, Apr.-Oct., Tue-Sun 11-18. Although discovered almost 100 years ago, excavations did not commence on the "villa rustica" until 1987. This 7.5 ha estate consisted of a villa, living quarters, farm buildings, bath, tavern an gardens. Today the roman villa has been reconstructed to its original condition. A small museum displays finds from the site. Meals are prepared in the tavern according to the cook book of the roman master chef Apicius (✆ 06865/9117-12).

Roman villa in Perl-Borg

Important: The excavation site is not located in Perl, but about 5 km outside, between Borg and Oberleuken. Moreover the route is very steep.

The Moselle River flows as a wide stream through its valley whose gentle slopes are clothed in vineyards and tall forests. The River also forms the border between Germany and Luxembourg. The communities of Perl (Ger), Schengen (Lux) and Apach (F) form the cross-border tourist region known as the "Schengener Eck".

The main route of the Moselle bike trail follows the right bank from Perl to Trier. Those wishing to experience a bit of Luxembourg should follow the route along the left bank from Schengen. You ride through the town of Remich, which entices you with its French flair to a stop in one of the many Cafés. After Wasserbillig you cross the Sauer river into Germany and soon arrive in Igel, home of the famous Igel Column. Finally you reach the legendary city of Trier, where it is possible to experience 2000 years of history with 2000 steps. The Romans chose this place for their seat of Government and built the famous Porta Nigra, a city gate of mammoth proportions. The Amphitheatre, Emperial Baths and the numerous palaces in the surrounding area bear witness to this important epoch.

The Moselle River Trail continues along paved bicycle paths and lanes with no significant inclines. Those riding with children should remain on the right bank however, as a longer section on the left bank route follows a bicycle lane along a busy road.

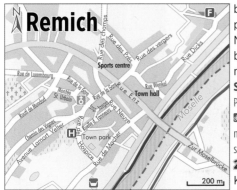

Remich

Sports centre

Town hall

Moselle

Town park

200 m

Schengen (Lux)/Perl   see page 33

Schengen/Perl
to Wormeldange   **19.5 km**

1 At the end of the bridge follow the right bend in the street ～ after a short distance a bicycle path begins on the right hand side of the road ～ follow the bicycle path along the Moselle out of Schengen ～ you pass under the freeway

bridge ～ the bicycle path soon reaches the N 10 and you follow the bicycle path along the main road northwards.

Schwebsange (Lux)

Postal code: 5447; Area code: 00352

🏕 **Camping/Port**, Route National 10, ✆ 26665956, (RentaBike, see page 8).

2 Continue past Bech-Kleinmacher.

Bech-Kleinmacher (Lux)

Continue along the bicycle path to Remich.

Remich (Lux)

Postal code: 5533; Area code: 00352

ℹ **Syndicat d'Initiative et Tourisme Remich**, 4 Rue Enz, ✆ 23698488

⚓ **Moselle river cruises**, Navitours, ✆ 758489.

🚌 **Gare routière Réimech**, Esplanade Moselle, ✆ 621356137, (RentaBike, see page 8)

Remich with its many cafés and bistros along the wide Esplanade

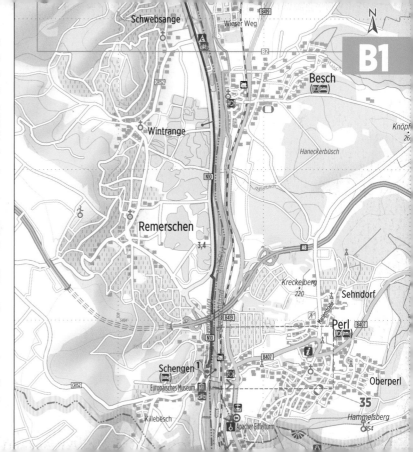

35

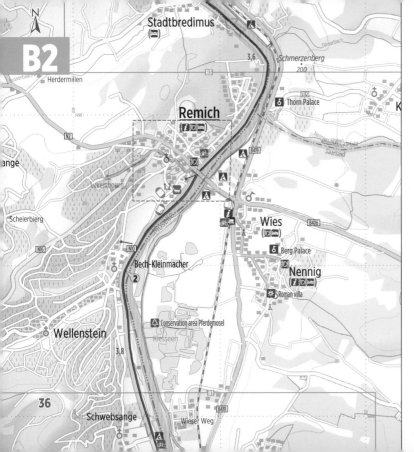

along the river front exudes French flair, and provides a fine setting to relax and watch the river traffic pass the town.

The bicycle path continues between the Moselle and the N 10 towards Stadtbrediums.

Stadtbrediums (Lux)

Postal code: 5450; Area code: 00352

🚲 **Hôtel de l'Ecluse**, 29, Waistroos, route du Vin, ✆ 2361911, (RentaBike, see page 8)

Follow the Moselle out of Stadtbrediums ⌇ the bicycle path becomes a bicycle lane, after a short distance on both sides of the road ⌇ continue along the bicycle lane along the **N 10** past Hettermillen to Ehnen.

Ehnen (Lux)

Postal code: 5416; Area code: 00352

🏛 🚲 **Maison et Musée du Vin**, 115, route du Vin, ✆ 760026, Open: Apr.-Oct., Tue-Sun 9:30-11:30 and 14-17, Nov.-Mar. and by arrangement.

Wine museum with bicycle rental (RentaBike, see page 8).

3 In Ehnen turn right immediately after the bridge and follow the bicycle path along the river bank ⌇ the bicycle path ends again and you continue on the bicycle lane along the **N 10** into Wormeldange ⌇ you pass under the road bridge.

Wormeldange (Lux)

Postal code: 5481; Area code: 00352

🚲 **Caves des Crémants Poll-Fabaire**, 115, route du Vin, ✆ 768211, (RentaBike, see page 8)

Wormeldange lies on the Luxembourgian Route du Vin and includes its largest and most famous vineyards, which cover some 1,465 hectares of land. The limy soils and sunny exposure allow these vineyards to produce an outstanding Riesling.

Ehnen

Wormeldange to Wasserbillig   17 km

Follow the bicycle lane along the main street out of Wormeldange and on to **4** Ahn.

Ahn (Lux)

Continue on the bicycle lane along the main road to **Machtum** ∿ after passing the village a bicycle path begins on the right hand side of the road ∿ continue to Grevenmacher.

Grevenmacher (Lux)

Postal code: 6794; Area code: 00352

🛈 **Syndicat d'Initiative Grevenmacher**, 10, route du Vin, ✆ 758275, www.grevenmacher.lu

🚢 **Moselle river cruises**, 10, route du Vin, ✆ 758275. The ships sail between Schengen and Wasserbillig.

🏛 **Kulturhuef**, 54 rte de Trèves, ✆ 4641, Museum, cinema and café.

⛪ **Chapel of the cross** (1737), sits

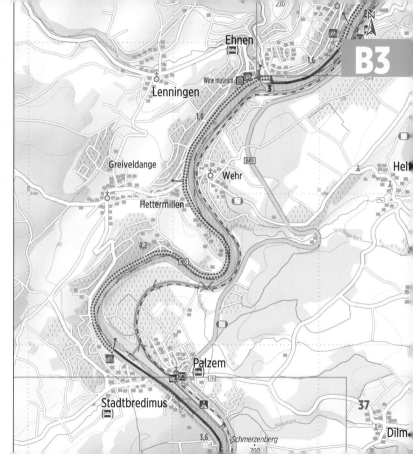

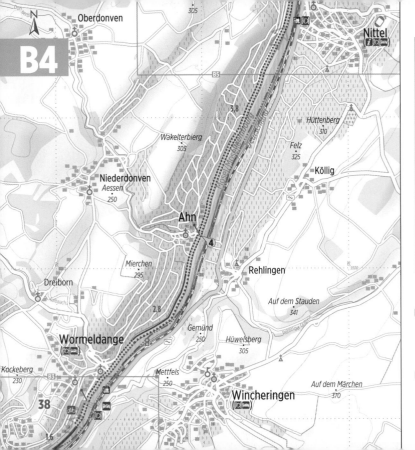

Oberdonven

Nittel

B5

3,8

Wakelterbierg
305

Hüttenberg
310

Niederdonven

Aessen
250

Felz
325

Köllig

Ahn

4

Mierchen
295

Rehlingen

Dreiborn

Auf dem Stauden
341

2,8

Gemünd
250

Hüwelsberg
305

Wormeldange

Mettfels
250

Auf dem Märchen
370

Kockeberg
230

B5

Wincheringen

38

1,6

N
Grevenmacher

Kulturhuef

Rue de Wecker

R. d. Muns

Butterflygarden

Sporthalle

Rue de la Tour

🛈 Chapel
of the Cross

Kohlenberg

Bernhard Massard

An der Gaarын

Route du Vin

LA MOSELLE

B 419

200 m

atop the "Kräizerbierg", from where you can
enjoy a wonderful view of the town.

⚹ **Bernard Massard sparkling wine cellars**,
☎ 750545228, Open: Apr.-Oct., Mon-Sun 9:30-
18. Slide show, cellar tour and sparkling wines
tasting.

⚹ **Butterfly garden**, ☎ 758539, Open: Apr.-
15th Oct., daily 9:30-17:30.

✉ **Outdoor pool**, 4 Kurzacht,
☎ 75821420

🚲 **Grevenmacher Camping**, route du Vin, ☎ 750234, (RentaBike,
see page 8)

*Grevenmacher is the
seat of Luxembourg's
oldest wine-coope-
rative. It was found-
ed in 1921, the same
year as the Bernard
Massard winery. The-
se sparkling wines are
made according to the
Champagne method.
It requires that each
bottle be treated with great care,
including the periodic turning of
the bottles.*

5 The bicycle path leaves the road
shortly after entering Grevenmacher and takes you under the
road bridge ⌇ continue along
the river bank past the outdoor

pool ∿ turn left between the pool and the tennis courts ∿ **6** turn right to continue on the bicycle path, which takes youn along the right side of the main road out of Grevenmacher ∿ you ride through an underpass before passing close to a harbour facility ∿ **7** after passsing the harbour turn right just before a small stream ∿ follow the bicycle path under the railway line and along the stream ∿ as you reach the harbour basin turn left across the bridge ∿ turn right immediately after the bridge and ride down to the Moselle in Mertert.

Wasserbillig

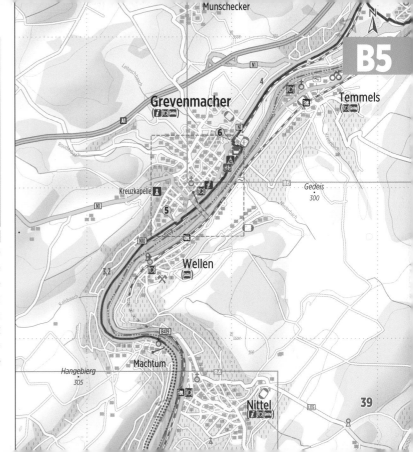

Mertert (Lux)

Follow the street along the river ∿ after a short distance keep right into the bicycle path ∿ follow the path along the Moselle until you reach the ferry at Wasserbillig. Just ahead of you lies the confluence of the Sauer and the Moselle rivers.

B5

Wasserbillig (Lux)

- **Ferry to Oberbillig** in Germany. Operates: Summer; Mon-Fri 7-20, Sat, Sun/Hol. 9-20. Winter; Mon-Fri 7-19.
- ✳ **Aquarium**, rue des Pépinières, Promenade de la Sûre, ✆ 26740237, Easter-Sept., daily 10-18, Oct.-Easter, Fri, Sat, Sun/Hol 10-17. Aquarium with salt water basins.

Wasserbillig to Trier   14 km

Just after the ferry landing cross the street and turn into the bicycle and pedestrian path ∼ follow the path through the railway underpass and up to the T-intersection ∼ turn right and cross the bridge over the Sauer River to Germany.

Wasserbilligerbrück

Postal code: 54308; Area code: 06501

- ℹ️ 🚲 **German-Luxembourgian Tourist-Information**, Langsur-Wasserbilligerbrück, Moselstr. 1, ✆ 602666, www.lux-trier.info, (RentaBike, see page 8)

Turn right after the bridge, where the road to the left leads to Langsur, and ride on the bicycle lane along the **B 49** ∼ a paved bicycle path begins on the right soon after passing below the railway bridge ∼ follow the path along the Moselle.

> **TIP** After a while you pass the village of Igel to your left, where the UNESCO world heritage listed Igeler Säule (Igel Column) makes it well worth a visit.

Igel

- ✳ **Igeler Säule (Igel Column)**. An originally preserved Roman grave monument.

*Igel is the home of one especially noteworthy object – the so-called **Igeler Säule**. This 23-meter obelisk was erected in the 3rd century by the brothers Lucius Secundinius Aventinus and Lucius Secundinius Securus in the name of their ancestors. The brothers were descendants of*

Trier, Kurfürstliches Palais

Celtic trevers who owned land that they leased to tenants. The rents were paid in cloth, which they could sell at city markets. Although they were legally Romans, they dressed and spoke in the dialect used by their kin. The wealthy family's villa, and presumably their graves, were on the hill where the village church stands today. The pillar honored the importance that textile making played. Its elaborate reliefs illustrate the craft, but also symbolize according to ancient mythology the passage of mortals and the well-earned elevation of their souls to heaven. The edifice survived because during the middle ages it was interpreted as represen-

Mesenich

Zewener Wald

Zewen

Liersberg

Oberkirc

Parish church

Langsur

Wollefsmillen

Saar

Sauertal-Radweg

Schaeferreder

Aquarium

Wasserbillig

B849

Igel

Mierchen

Grand Rue

Haus der Fischerei

Wasserbilligerbrück

Wasserbilligbrück

Mosel

Moselle

5,2

Roman coloumn

Former mor

Syr

N1

3,4

Oberbillig

B7

8

Mertert

Wasserliesch

B849

schecker

Syr

7

Reinig

N1

4

B5

Konz

i

Temmels

N1

6

Fellerich

Rosenberg

Könen

B51

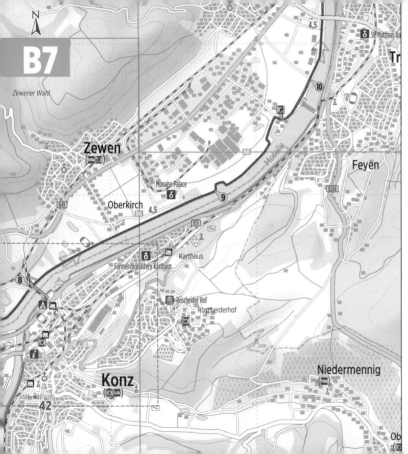

Zewener Wald

Zewen

Feyen

Oberkirch

Monaise Palace

Former monastery Karthaus

Karthaus

Roscheider Hof
Roscheiderhof

Niedermennig

Konz

Konzer Bach

42

...ting the marriage of the Empress Helena to Constantius Chlorus. Because Helena was considered a saint, the images on the pillar were interpreted in a Christian fashion. The pillar's significance was not correctly understood until the 16th century.

Continue on the bicycle path along the river ~ the river has become wider since passing Wasserbillig and now swells as it also takes the water from the Saar River, which flows into the Moselle on the opposite bank ~ after the confluence of the Saar and the Moselle the town of Konz comes into view ~ **8** you pass under a railway bridge.

CENTRE Turn left after riding under the bridge to reach Konz or to change to the route on the opposite bank of the river.

Continue along the river ~ after a while the Monaise Villa comes into view.

Schloss Monaise (Monaise Villa)

The villa's renovation was completed in 1997. It was built by Francois Ignace Mangin between 1779 and 1783, as the summer residence for the cathedral provost Nikolaus von Walderdorff. From outside the villa resembles the north Italian country villas built by Andrea

Trier

Palladio. The interior was finished with an eye more to comfort than beauty, a fact reflected by its name, which roughly means "my comfort."

9 A short distance after the villa ride to the left around the small marina ⁓ after another kilometer a fence blocks the way. There is a shipyard behind the buildings and you must ride to the left around the facility ⁓ turn right after the shipyard and you quickly reach the Moselle again before passing a barrage and lock ⁓ **10** ride past the turnoff towards Trier-Euren and continue toward the centre of Trier ⁓ pass under the first bridge ⁓ after about 1 km you reach the Römerbrücke.

Römerbrücke (Roman Bridge)

Five of the original nine Roman pylons can be seen today and date from the 2nd century AD, making it the oldest bridge in Germany. Originally the stone pylons carried a wooden bridge construction 14 m above the water, which was not replaced by stone vaulting until the middle ages, being renewed in 1718 after being blown up by French troops in 1689.

A little further down stream you may notice two round buildings on the opposite bank. Looking somewhat like old windmills, they are in fact old cranes which had been used to load and unload ships.

Continue along the river to the **Kaiser-Wilhelm-Brücke 1**.

CENTRE You can cross the Moselle on the Kaiser-Wilhelm-Brücke to reach the centre of Trier

Trier

Postal code: 54290; Area code: 0651

ℹ Tourist-Information, at the Porta Nigra, ☎ 978080, www.trier.de

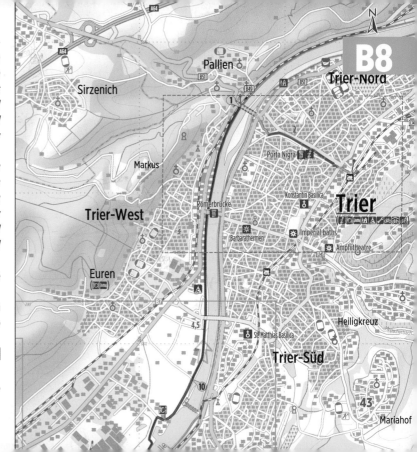

B8

Trier – Amphitheater

🚢 **Moselle river cruises:** Trier-Bernkastel and back as well as to Cochem and Koblenz. Personenschifffahrt Kolb, Operates: May-Nov., Tue, Thur, Sat, Sun/Hol. 9am from the passenger ship harbor, ✆ 26666 or Tourist Information Trier.

🏛 **Rheinisches Landesmuseum (State museum),** Weimarer Allee 1, ✆ 97740, Open: Tue-Sun 10-17:30. This museum displays archaeological artifacts and artworks from the Moselle region, from prehistoric through Roman to the early modern era.

🏛 **Museum am Dom Trier (Episcopal museum),** Bischof-Stein-Platz 1, ✆ 7105255, Open: Apr.-Oct., Mon-Sat 9-17, Sun/Hol. 13-17, Nov.-Mar., Tue-Sat 9-17, Sun/Hol. 13-17. Collection of church art belonging to the diocese of Trier, including early Christian artifacts and Roman ceiling paintings.

🏛 **Stadtmuseum Simeonstift (Town museum),** Simeonstr. 60, ✆ 7181459 or 7181454, Open: Tue-Sun, 10 - 18

🏛 **Domschatzkammer (Cathedral treasury),** Hohe Domkirche, ✆ 9790790, Open: Apr.-Oct./Dec., Mon-Sat 10-17, Sun/Hol 12:30-17, Nov/Jan.-Mar., Tue-Sat 11-16, Sun/Hol. 14-16. Goldsmiths art from the 10th-19th c., including liturgical items and writings decorated with precious artwork.

🏛 **Stadtbibliothek (City library),** Weberbach 25, ✆ 7182430, Open: Mon, Wed, Fri 9-13, Tue, Thur 9-17. Gutenberg bible, old documents, certificates, baroque globes and historic maps.

🏛 **Karl-Marx-Haus (Karl Marx's birthplace),** Brückenstr. 10, ✆ 970680, Open: Apr.-Oct., daily 10-18, Nov.-Mar., Tues-Sun 11-17, Mon 14-17. Birthplace of the founder of modern socialism.

🏛 **Spielzeugmuseum (Toy museum),** Hauptmarkt, ✆ 75850, Open: Jan.-Mar., Tue-Sun 11-17, Apr.-Dec., daily 11-18. Metal toys, trains, dolls and dollhouses, shops, teddy bears, rocking horses and much more.

Trier – Porta Nigra

✝ **Cathedral,** ✆ 9790790, Open: Nov.-Mar., 6:30-17:30, Apr.-Oct., 6:30-18. Oldest parts from the 4th c., Romanesque west wing.

✝ **St. Paulin,** Open: Mar.-Sept., Mon, Wed, Sat 9-18, Tue 11-18, Sun 10-18, Oct.-Feb., Mon, Wed, Sat 9-17, Tue 11-17, Sun 10-17. Baroque church built according to plans by Balthasar Neumann.

✝ **St.-Matthias Basilica,** the grave of St. Matthias has been venerated here since the 12th c.

✝ **Konstantin Basilica/Aula Palatina,** Open: Apr.-Oct., Mon-Sat 10-18, Sun/holidays 12-18, Nov.-Mar., Tue-Sat 11-12 and 15-16, Son/Hol. 12-13, no admittance 30 mins before closing time. Roman palace hall, today a protestant church, with Roman throne room 67 m long, 27 m wide and 30 m high.

✳ **Roman sites,** Open: Apr.-Sept., 9-18, Oct., Mar., 9-17, Nov.- Feb., 9-16.

✳ **Porta Nigra,** Roman city gate, 2nd century AD.

✳ **Amphitheatre,** built 100 AD, with capacity for 20,000 spectators.

✳ **Barbarathermen (Barbara baths),** Roman baths complex from the 2nd century AD.

✳ **Kaiserthermen (Imperial baths),** large Roman baths palace, 4th century AD.

✳ **Medieval sights: Frankenturm** (11th century), Dietrichstraße, **Dreikönigenhaus** (13th century), Simonstraße.

Trier

Maria Königin

Maria Königin

St. Martin
St. Martin Abbey
Barmherzige Brüder Hospital
Elisabeth Hospital

St. Paulin

Mariahilf Chapel

St. Maximin

Porta Nigra
Town museum

Weiße Väter

St. Paulus

St. Irmin Monastery
Monastery
Anna Abbey

St. Gangolf

Episcopal museum
Cathedral
Walderdorf Palace
Resselstatt Palace
Liebfrauen Church

Train station

St. Josef

Karl Marx's birthplace

Jesuit Church

Konstantin Basilica
Electoral Palace

State museum

Town theatre
Town hall
Europahalle

Moselle

Römerbrücke

45

200 m

Trier – Hauptmarkt

❈ **Kurfürstlicher Palast (Electoral palace)**, Rococo palace from the 18th century designed by Johannes Seiz. Includes interior artwork by the Bohemian sculptor F. Tietz, the stucco plasterer M. Extel from Tyrol and the painters J. Zick and J. Zauffally.

❈ **Educational tour "Interesting and amazing facts about the cultivation and growth of the grape vine."** An educational path around the Petrisberg (near the amphitheatre), Open: daily year-round.

🚲♿ **Bürgerservice GmbH**, Bahnsteig 1, ☎ 148856

🚲 **Henn Zweiräder**, Viehmarktpl. 17, ☎ 73382

🚲 **Fahrrad Lauter**, Paulinstr. 32, ☎ 27669

🚲 **Bicycle garage**, near Tourist Info/Porta Nigra, info., ☎ 978080, **Bicycle boxes** at the messepark.

A slogan for the town claims it is possible to see 2,000 years of history in 2,000 paces in Trier. There is hardly another town in Germany where the ancient roots of middle-European and occidental culture at the intersection of the Roman and Germanic zones of influence have been so impressively preserved. Survey more than 2,000 years of history during a walking tour through Trier.

Start at the Porta Nigra, this truly imperial Roman gate. Its monumental architecture embodies the Roman empire's dreams of eternal strength and power. After the fall of the empire, a hermit named Simeon, who was close to the bishop Poppo, moved into the gate, which was transformed into a double church that made use of the entire gate.

To the west of the Porta Nigra stands the Simeonstift, a monastery with its two-story cloister, one of the most beautiful monuments of early-Romanesque cloister architecture. It was founded in 1034 by Archbishop Poppo. Across the Simeonstraße, which was laid out according to a plan dating from Roman times,

you quickly come to the main market. Along the route, you pass the Dreikönigenhaus. This superb example of Romanesque defensive and residential architecture dates to the 13th century. The late-gothic Steipe was originally built about 200 years later, and had to be rebuilt from the ruins of World War II. This ensemble of facades representing various periods stands next to the massive St. Gangolf church, the old 10th century market junction and the Petrus fountain dating from the Renaissance.

Branching off to the right from the market is the Dietrichstraße, one of Trier's delightful narrow city streets and the location of ano-

Trier, Kaiserthermen

ther Romanesque jewel, the Frankenturm. The Sternstraße leads to the Domfreihof, which is dominated by the early Romanesque cathedral, the early-gothic Liebfrauenkirche and the baroque Palais Kesselstatt. The rich ornamentation of the cathedral, the priceless objects in the treasure-chamber, and the epitaphs of famous church figures and other dignitaries represent a concentration of art and history the significance of which extends far beyond Trier itself. The cathedral and the Liebfrauenkirche are connected by a cloister from which the sublime interplay of architectural styles evident in the two churches can be appreciated.

From here it is just a short walk to the basilica, the core of which is the Aula Palatina built in 310 AD by the emperor Constantine. In the 4th century Roman emperors ruled their realm from this impressive 30 m tall edifice. Adjacent to the basilica to the south is the Kurfürstliche, or elector's, palace. The opulent rococo facade was designed by Johannes Seiz, a pupil of Balthasar Neumann.

Trier, Matthias Basilika

Through the palace garden, with its many flower beds, lawns and hedges providing the background for numerous statues, one soon comes to the ruins of the imperial baths. If one follows the Olewiger Straße to the foot of the Petrisberg, one reaches the amphitheater with its oval arena and rows of seating. In Roman times up to 20,000 spectators could come here to watch gladiators and wild animals battle to the death.

A tour of Trier would not be complete without a visit to the old townhouse in the Brückenstraße 10. This is where Karl Marx was born on May 5, 1818. Today it houses a museum that holds a collection of Marx's writings and correspondence, and documents the life and accomplishments of "the father of scientific socialism."

ALTERNATIVE Here in Trier you now have the alternative option of boarding a cruise ship near the Kaiser Wilhelm Bridge to continue part of your journey down the Moselle river on the water.

Perl/Schengen to Trier on the right bank

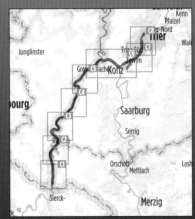

The main route of the Moseele river trail follows the right bank from Perl to Trier. Excursions in the first few kilometres entice you to taking in the Berg Palace, a Roman mosaic with 161 square metres or Thorn Palace. You continue to Konz, which lies on the confluence of the Saar and Moselle Rivers and where the remains of a Roman imperial villa can be seen. You pass the Karthaus Monastery, the St. Matthias Basilica and the Roman Bridge before reaching the Kaiser Wilhelm Bridge in Trier, from where you can take an excursion into the historic city centre, where numerous Roman sights and museums await you.

This mostly flat route takes you along paved bicycle paths and quiet side streets, so that one can enjoy the ride almost free from motorised traffic..

Perl

Perl to Nittel   **25.2 km**

1 Continue straight past the train station ∼ turn left under a railway line and continue directly beside the Moselle ∼ the railway lines are now to the right of the bicycle path ∼ follow the paved route ∼ **2** keep left at the fork in the road and ride along the Moselle ∼ the houses of Besch are on the right.

Besch

The route turns right, away from the river ∼ **3** turn left at the intersection and return to the Moselle ∼ follow the towpath along the river.

You now pass through the ornitological reserve "Pferdemosel", which developed from an old arm of the river and numerous former gravel pits. Numerous rare bird species find refuge and breed here, and the ponds are also used for angling.

The route passes the "Dreiländereck" camping ground.

EXCURSION Just before you reach the bridge turn right towards Nenning. This wine growers village is famous for the roman villa with its most impressive mosaics north of the Alps.

To the Roman Villa and Berg Palace   **4 km**

Keep right at the roundabout ∼ take the first street left towards the village ∼ straight ahead then left by the stop sign ∼ in the curve turn left towards the palace or turn right towards the roman villa.

TIP At the palace you can visit the renaissance garden, one out of 25 gardens that belong to

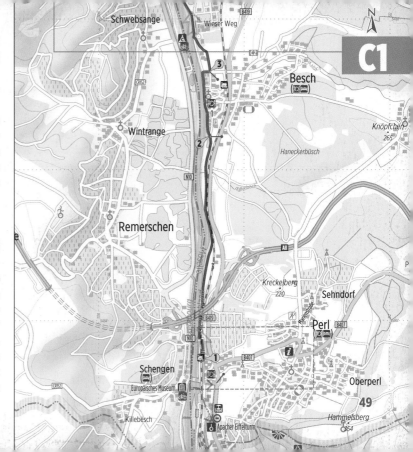

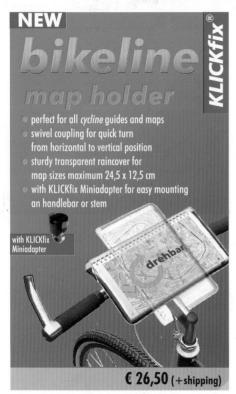

the cross-border project "gardens without borders".

Nennig

Postal code: 66706; Area code: 06866

🛈 **Verkehrsverein Nennig**, Bübinger Str. 5, ✆ 1439, www.nennig.de

🛏 **Berg Palace**. Today it houses a luxury hotel and casino. The Renaissance style palace gardens are open all year.

✳ **Roman villa and mosaic**, Römerstr., ✆ 1329, Open: Apr.-Sept., Tue-Sun 9-18, Mar., Oct., Nov., Tue-Sun 9-16. The Roman villa complex houses the largest Roman mosaic north of the Alps. It dates from the 2nd or 3rd c. AD.

🚲 **Verkehrsverein Nennig**, train station, ✆ 1439

"Mosella resplendent as for a feast, embraced from left and right by palaces," wrote Decimus Magnus Ausonius, tutor to Gratianus in the 4th century AD. One of the most magnificent of these palaces was discovered near Nennig. Excavations brought to light not only insights into Roman life and engineering, but also a masterful mosaic.

The 161 m2 floor mosaic creates the illusion of a carpet lying on marble tiles. This "carpet" consists of almost 3 million small colored

Berg palace in Nennig

stones, or about 175 stones per square decimeter. The individual images appear to depict scenes from an amphitheater's program. The program opens with music, shown in an image of two musicians with an organ and a horn. The largest picture shows the terrible main act in which the "secutor" and the "retiarius" face each other. Other acts include men overpowering a bear, a tiger that has brought down a donkey, and an animal trainer. The final scene shows an old animal keeper pushing a tame lion out of the arena after it has finished devouring the slain animals.

The Route along the Moselle passes under the B 406, then passes the **4** camping ground "Mosella"  follow the paved route along the river and pass by a camping ground again  right of you there are railway tracks and the B 419.

EXCURSION About 1 km after the bridge over the Moselle there is a railway underpass on the right. From here you can get to the wine-growing estate and palace "Schloss Thorn". This palace is privately owned.

Schloss Thorn (Thorn Palace)

The grounds surrounding Schloss Thorn date back to the middle ages, though only the gate tower remain from those times. The lords of Rollingen, Luxembourgian nobility, owned the property originally. They were followed by the Lords of Bübingen.

Mosel near Thorn palace

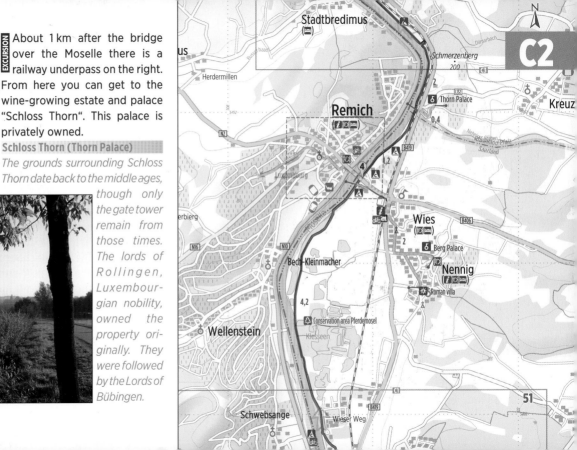

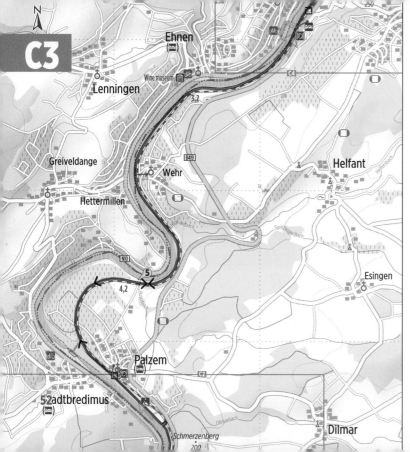

The House of Musiel held the castle from the 16th to the 19th centuries. Members of this family collected from the surrounding fields artifacts from Frankish times. This famous collection is now on exhibit in the Landesmuseum (state museum) in Trier.

The border between the German states of Saarland, which you now leave, and Rhineland-Palatinate, runs just beyond Schloss Thorn.

ATTENTION One consequence is that the signs that mark the bicycle route along the Moselle change their appearance. The new sign is white, with the familiar "M" for Moselle now shown in green.

Continue to Palzem between the Moselle and the railway tracks.

Palzem

The town's name evolved from Palatiolum, which translates roughly as "small palace." There was a bridge over the Moselle here as early as 50 BC, built not by the Romans but by the Celts.

Continue straight at the small intersection and keep riding beside the railroad tracks ⁓ **5** the route reaches the Moselle again, so that it runs once more between river and railway ⁓ pass by the village Wehr.

Wehr

Follow the route between the river and the railway ⁓ pass by the train station of Wincheringen

TIP By Wincheringen it is possible to get to Luxembourg by crossing the bridge over the Moselle.

Wincheringen

The path bends left and right and takes you over a stone bridge ⁓ continue parallel to the Moselle ⁓ **6** keep left at the fork in the path, there is a barrier and railway crossing on the right ～ pass the train station of Nittel.

Nittel

Postal code: 54453; Area code: 06584

View over Temmels

ℹ Heimat- und Verkehrsverein, Weinstr. 24, 📞 99360, www.nittel-mosel.de

The town claims that 2 million, mostly Elbling, grape vines grow in its immediate vicinity. They produce a simple but fresh and somewhat dry wine. Nittel itself lies on the river at the foot of a massive dolomite cliff that the river loops around.

Nittel to Konz   15.5 km

Continue between river and railway ～ ride under the B 419 ～ the route is now on the right side of the road ～ the bicycle path leads towards Wellen.

Wellen

Turn away from the main road to the right into **Moselstraße** ～ follow this street through the village of Wellen ～ continue on the right side of the main road ～ pass by the train station ～ **7** cross the intersection at the bridge ～ you ride under the main road to the

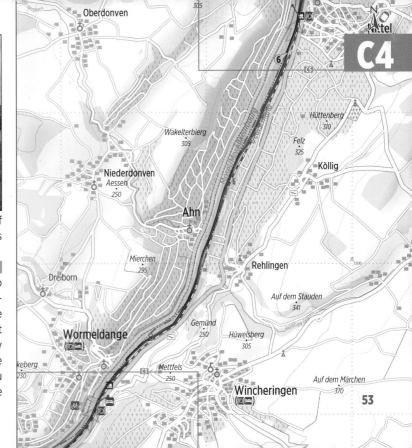

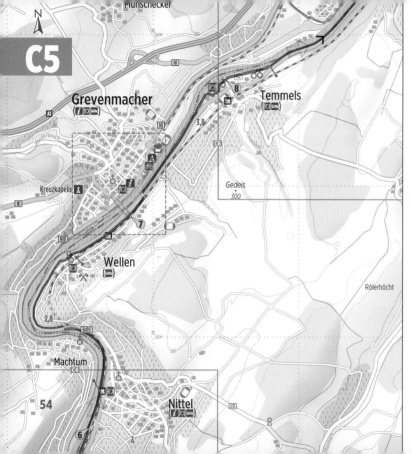

Grevenmacher

Temmels

Kreuzkapelle

Gedeis
300

Wellen

Rölerhöcht

Machtum

54

Nittel

left soon after the bridge ∼ the bicycle path again runs just beside the river ∼ at the T-intersection turn left towards Temmels.

Temmels

Follow the street into the village ∼ ride straight at the intersection ∼ at the T-intersection by the memorial turn right into **Mosel- straße** ∼ **8** turn left at the next T-intersection, the route goes back to the Moselle ∼ and you ride out of Temmels ∼ at the fork in the road keep left ∼ straight towards Oberbillig, left of the main road.

Oberbillig

- ⛴ **Ferry to Wasserbillig,** Operates: summer: Mon-Fri 7-20, Sat, Sun/Hol 9-20; winter: Mon-Fri 7-19, Sat, Sun/Hol 10-19.
- ✷ **House of Fishing and Fishing Museum with fish store,** Moselstr. 45, ☎ 9698730. Restau-

Roman imperial villa Konz

rant and overnight accommodation. The multi-media fishing museum describes history and development of the region's fishing industry.

The bicycle path leads onto a small street, which you follow all the way to the ferry ∼ a narrow bicycle path goes off to the left before the village street starts climbing toward the main road ∼ this path takes you along the riverbank to Konz ∼ **9** you leave the water for a short distance as the bicycle path

Mesenich

Zewener Wald

Zewen

Parish church
Langsur
Wollefsmillen
Liersberg
Monaise Palace
Oberkirch

Schaeferreder
Aquarium
Wasserbillig
Sauertal-Radweg

B49
Moselle
Igel
Karthaus
Former monastery Karthaus

Grand Rue
Wasserbilligerbrück
Roman coloumn
Roscheider Hof
Roscheiderhof

Haus der Fischerei
Oberbillig

Mertert
Wasserliesch
Reinig
Konz

B49

Temmels

Fellerich
Rosenberg
Könen
55
Kommling

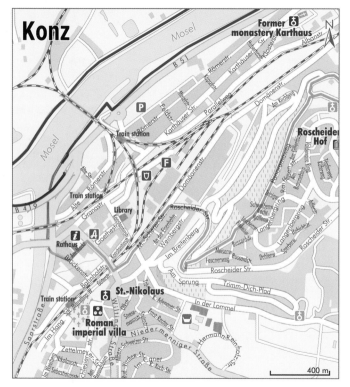

Konz

curves around the playing field at Wasserliesch.

Wasserliesch

You continue along the river bank until just before Saar-Moselle the confluence ∾ short ascent towards the bicycle path on the road bridge ∾ cross the Saar ∾ at the end of the bridge follow the bicycle path through the underpass back to the Moselle ∾ by the river bank turn right to continue.

CENTRE To reach the centre of Konz and to connect to the alternative route via Konz turn left by the river bank and follow the orange route marked in the map.

Konz

Postal code: 54329; Area code: 06501

i **Saar-Obermosel-Touristik e.V.,** Granastr. 22, ☎ 6018040, www.saar-obermosel.de

🏛 **Folklore and open-air museum Roscheider Hof,** located above Konz, ☎ 92710, Open: Apr.-Oct., Tue-Fri 9-18, Sat, Sun/Hol 10-18, Nov.-Mar., Tue-Fri 9-17, Sat, Sun/Hol 10-17. Exhibits on rural industries including iron-working, brewing, laundry and winemaking.

🏰 **Former monastery Karthaus** (17th c.), Brunostr. 23

🏛 **Roman imperial villa** (4th c.), near St. Nikolaus Church

Konz is the former Contoniacum, the summer residence of the Roman Emperor Valentian I, who was responsible for the western part of the empire from 364 to 375 AD. Unfortunately little of the emperor's villa remains.

The Roscheider Hof offers rather more to see. A Benedictine farm was started here in the 14th century. Around the farm grew a picturesque village on the valley's sloping side. Various workshops, a school house and even a grocer have been accurately recreated, including antique furnishings. A stroll through this museum transports the visitor into

Konz, Roscheider Hof

the slower, simpler world that our ancestors knew.

Konz to Trier   *9.5 km*

Continue along the right bank of the Moselle ～ circle around a small harbour ～ pass the ruins of the Karthaus Monastery complex.

Former monastery Karthaus

The tall, narrow-single-nave curch forms the central axis of the com-plex. The facade of red sands-tone with its two gables loom above the roof. The facade is dominated by the two over-sized figures of St. Bruno and St. Franziskus.

Continue between the river and the railway line towards Trier ～ **10** ride past Konrad Adenauer Bridge, from which a street leads to a mighty church, the St. Matthias basilica.

St. Matthias Basilica

This basilica was initially built due to the presence of a roman

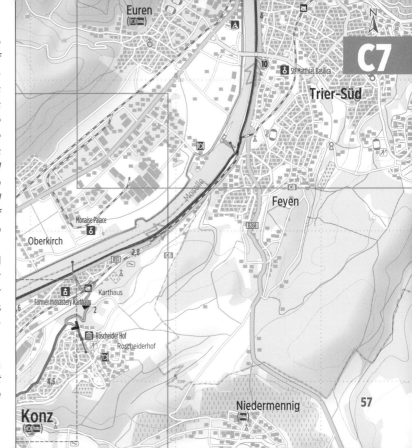

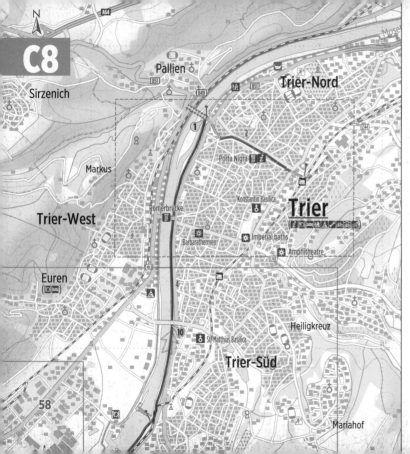

Sirzenich

Pallien

Trier-Nord

Markus

Porta Nigra

Konstantin Basilica

Trier

Trier-West

Römerbrücke

Barbarathermen

Imperial baths

Amphitheatre

Euren

Heiligkreuz

St. Matthias Basilica

Trier-Süd

Mariahof

burial ground. Eucharius, the first bishop of Trier, built a church on the site, which he dedicated to the evangelist John. He and his successor, Valerius, were buried there. This "Cella Euchari i" was destroyed by the Franks. About 460 AD, bishop Cyrillus built a new church nearby and moved the relics there.

During this period a community of clerics moved into the area. When the current basilica was built in 1127, the relics of the apostle Matthew were found, making the site not only the final resting place of bishops, but a destination for countless pilgrims. Over time the new name, St. Matthias, was adopted. When the basilica was consecrated by Pope Eugene III in 1148, not less than 47 cardinals attended – a testimony to the site's importance at the time.

Continue along the bank of the Moselle ~ pass below the bridge Römerbrücke ~ continue to the **Kaiser-Wilhelm-Brücke 1**.

> **TIP** If you want to continue your tour on the other side of the river, cross the Moselle here.

Trier   **see page 43**

Trier to Bernkastel-Kues on the left bank

65 km

You leave the impressive city of trier behind and make your way towards Bernkastel-Kues. Along the next 65 kilometres you can, amongst many other attractions, make an excursion to Ramstein Castle, see the ferry tower in Schweich or visit the Roman wine press from the 3rd and 4th century in Piesport. In Bernkastel-Kues you may not want to miss trying the legendary "Bernkastler Doctor".

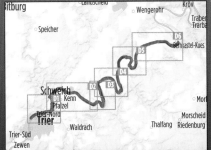

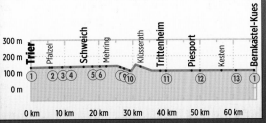

The flat route makes use of quiet streets, bicycle paths and bicycle lanes.

The official main route of the Moselle river trail follows the left bank from Trier to Schweich, where it changes to the right bank.

Trier see page 43

Trier to Mehring 21.5 km

1 Pass below the Kaiser-Wilhelm-Brücke and continue along the asphalt bicycle path beside the Moselle ~ the railway line runs to the left of your route for some time, before it turns away to the north ~ continue along the bicycle path ~ you ride below another railway bridge before coming into Pfalzel.

Pfalzel

This is a charming little town with historic houses that exhibit architectural styles ranging from the Gothic to the 20th century. The Kirchplatz (church square) features the oldest stone building in Germany. A short stroll through the narrow streets and squares is well worth it.

Ride through the gap in the flood protection wall ~ turn right, following the Moselle route signs towards Ehrang ~ you pass through the flood protection wall again and ride between walls ~ follow the street **An der Bastion** ~ you ride past the Hotel Klosterschenke and a part of the old stone ramparts.

To the left stand the remains of the town's ramparts, which were erected in the 16th century to protect its wealthy citizens.

Turn left into the next street, the **Hans-Adamy-Straße** ~ pass the sports facilities ~ at the next intersection turn right ~ ride along the **Mittelweg** ~ at the end of the houses follow the left bend into the **Karolingerstraße** ~ **2** opposite the next side street on the left follow the signs directing you to the right onto a bike path through a band of trees and over railway tracks ~ follow the bicycle path beside the railway tracks ~ cross the parking lot to reach the Hafenstraße ~ cross the street and turn right onto the bicycle path along the left side of the

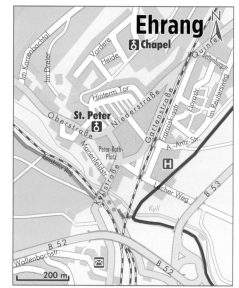

road ~ follow the bicycle path through the left bend in the road, where it becomes the **Am Moselkai** ~ in the left bend continue stright ahead ~ straight through the left side of the turning area at the end of the road ~ the bicycle path leads you to the embankment below the B 52 ~ where you turn right ~ follow the path to the river and turn left under the B 52 ~ keep left immediately after the bridge and follow the bicycle path away from the river ~ **3** you pass under another road bridge ~ follow the right bend in the path, which then takes you over a bridge across the little Kyll River.

Here you could turn left instead of right and follow the signs to Kordel and the Kylltalradweg (Kyll Valley Bicycle Trail) to take a trip into the Kyll Valley and the castle ruin of Ramstein.

Continue straight ahead on the path ~ you pass the Marien Hospital.

Ehrang

Continue straight along the paved bicycle path ~ to the left are the houses of Ehrang ~ just before the main road turn left into the bicycle and pedestrian path ~ then to the right under the road ~ follow the path after the underpass ~ turn right into the path which runs along an industrial building ~ follow the curve to the right ~ **4** you pass under the B 53 and keep left ~ by the river

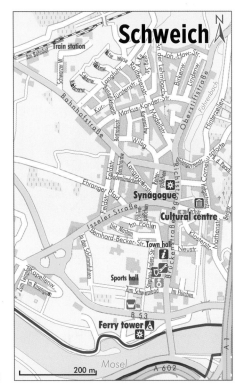

Schweich

N

Train station

Synagogue

Cultural centre

Town hall

Sports hall

Ferry tower

B 53

Mosel   A 602

200 m

bank turn left ∾ you pass the houses of **Issel** ∾ keep right at the fork in the road ∾ you continue along the bank of the river towards the town of Schweich ∾ follow the left-right curves in the path around a marina ∾ keep right and ride along the allee by the river ∾ to the left is a camping ground.

Schweich

Postal code: 54338; Area code: 06502

- 🛈 **Tourist-Information Römische Weintaße,** Brückenstr. 46, ☎ 93380, www.roemische-weinstrasse.de
- 🏛 **Kulturzentrum Niederprümer Hof,** Hofgartenstr. 26, ☎ 6524, Open: Tue 14-16 or by arrangement under ☎ 0176/39757716. Exhibits covering the life and work of the writer Stefan Andreas and Father Johannes Maria Haw. The top floor holds the "Leierkasten" puppet theatre.
- 🕎 **Synagogue,** cultural centre, Richtstr. 40, ☎ 933825, Open: Tue 10-12, Thur 14-16 or by arrangement under ☎ 0176/39757716.
- 🚲 **Rad & Fun Sport GbR,** Im Handwerkerhof 2, ☎ 937333

*The first you see of Schweich is a small marina and a camping ground built around the old **ferry tower**. The tower is a relic from the time when the ferry was the only way to cross the river.* Continue along the river bank after the camping ground ∾ you pass under a road bridge

Ferry tower Schweich

and continue stright ∾ cross a small bridge before passing below the freeway bridge ∾ turn left up to the main road ∾ cross the road and turn right onto the bicycle path along the left side of the **B 53** ∾ continue along the bicycle lane ∾ **5** you pass a bridge over the Moselle and continue towards Longen ∾ before reaching the village you turn right into a lane between the vinyards ∾ take the next lane to the left ∾ you pass through Longen.

Longen

Continue straight through the intersection ∾ you ride between vinyards ∾ turn right at the

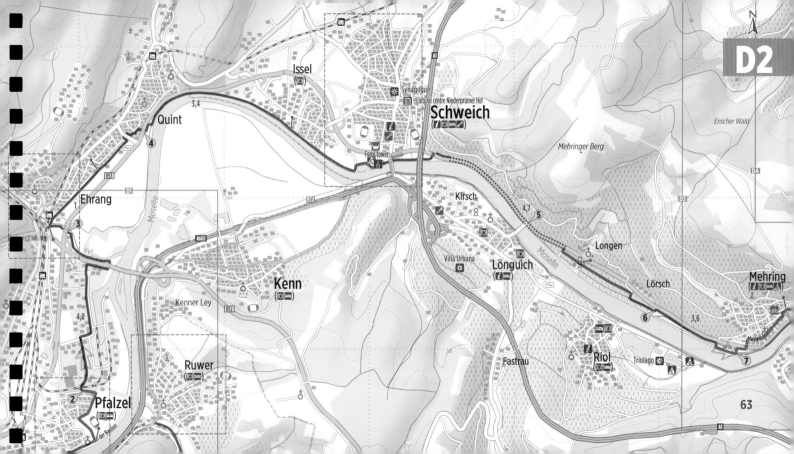

Enscher Wald

Issel

Synagogue
Cultural centre Niederprümer Hof
Schweich

Mehringer Berg

Quint

3,4

4

Ferry Tower

B53

Ehrang

1

Moselle

D1

L145

Kirsch

Longen

4,7

5

3

A602

Kyll

Villa Urbana

Longuich

Moselle

Lörsch

Mehring

Kenn

Kenner Ley

B52

6

3,6

4,2

Fastrau

Riol

Triolago

7

Medardusbrücke

Ruwer

2

Pfalzel

In der Bach.

A1

63

Mehring, Villa Rustica

T-intersection and then left at the next opportunity ～ **6** turn left at the next T-intersection and then to the right just before the main road ～ follow the lane parallel to the main road towards Mehring ～ turn right at the next T-intersection and you come to ride along the edge of the Moselle once again ～ **7** turn left into the street **Zellerhof** and follow it to the right along the main road ～ turn left across the main road into the **Bachstraße** ～ then immediately right into **Medarusstraße** ～ follow this street through Mehring.

Mehring

Postal code: 54346; Area code: 06502

- ℹ **Touristinformation Mehring,** Bachstr. 47, ✆ 1413, www.mehring-mosel.de
- 🏛 **Wine and Local History Museum**, Bachstr. 47, ✆ 1413
- ✳ **Villa Rustica (Roman villa)**, Remains and reconstruction of a Roman villa.
- 🚲 **Fahrradverleih Lonien**, Im Blumengarten 5, ✆ 8967

Mehring to Trittenheim   14.5 km

Continue to the T-intersection ～ turn left into the **Engelstraße** ～ then right onto the **Brückenstraße** ～ before the right bend in the road towards the bridge, continue straight into the **Gartenstraße** ～ this takes you in a right curve down to the main road B 53 ～ turn left and ride on the bicycle lane along the **B 53** ～ after rounding a tight bend in the river you approach Pölich ～ follow the route to the left away from the B 53 and into the village.

Pölich

Postal code: 54340; Area code: 06507

- ℹ **Tourist Information Pölich**, Hauptstr. 30, ✆ 3064, www.poelich-online.de

- 🏛 **Porta Libertas** (Roman Water Conduit, ca. 206 AD), well preserved Roman tunnel cut through the bedrock below the vinyards above Pölich. Once carried water to a bath complex.

Follow the street until you reach the tourist information ～ at the fork in the road here keep right ～ ride back to the B 53 and cross to the lane on the other side ～ turn left on the lane and continue past the first turnoff ～ **8** turn right at the second turnoff, the path straight ahead is unpaved ～ at the intersection turn left ～ continue through the vinyards and the left bend in the lane ～ at the T-intersection turn right ～ then left at the next T-intersection as you reach the houses of Schleich ～ **9** keep right at the fork in the road directly afterwards ～ continue on this street along the edge of Schleich.

Schleich

Continue straight along the street past the houses ～ follow the left bend in the street ～ turn right at the T-intersection ～ you once again ride along a lane between vinyards ～ **10** turn left immediately after crossing a small wooden bridge ～ turn right before the main road ～ and follow this lane beside the main road ～ continue to an intersection in front of an underpass below the main road.

Ensch

Turn left at the intersection and ride through the underpass ～ turn right immediately after the underpass ～ follow the street parallel to the main road along the edge of Ensch ～ at the end of the town follow the curve up to the main road and turn left ～ after a few hundred metres you come to ride on a bicycle path along the left side of the road ～ pass under the road bridge and continue towards Klüsserath ～ pass the first turnoff to the left ～ after the bridge over the Salm, turn left into Klüsserath ～ follow the right bend in the street.

Klüsserath

Postal code: 54340; Area code: 06507

🛈 Tourist Information, Kirchstr. 3, ✆ 3099, www.kluesserath.net

🏛 **Haus der Krippen (Crib museum)**, Hauptstr. 83, ✆ 939204, Open: Fri-Sun 14-18, Nov-2. Feb., Tue-Sun 14-18. Over 90 different cribs showing the birth of Jesus as well as background information.

Follow the **Mittelstraße** through the town ～ after passing the last houses ride to the main road and turn left onto the bicycle lane ～ continue all the way to Trittenheim.

Trittenheim

Postal code: 54349; Area code: 06507

Trittenheim

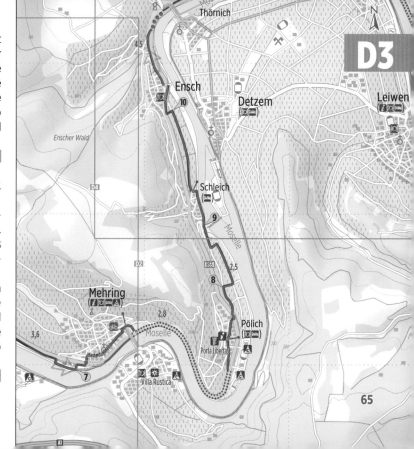

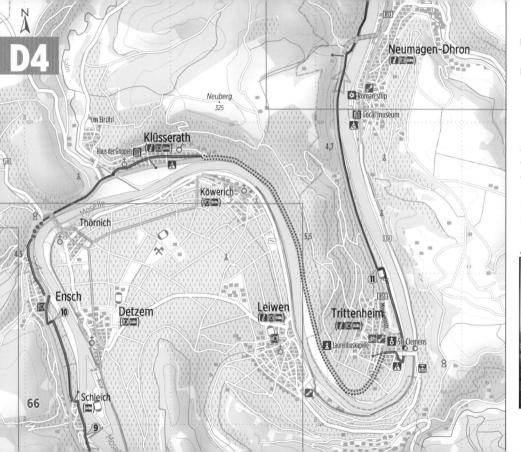

Neumagen-Dhron

Neuberg 325

Im Brühl

Klüsserath

Haus der Grippen

Köwerich

Thörnich

Moselle

Roman ship

Local museum

4,7

5,5

Ensch

10

Detzem

Leiwen

Trittenheim

11

Laurentiuskapelle

St. Clemens

Schleich

9

ℹ️ **Tourist-Information**, Moselweinstr. 55, ☎ 2227, www.trittenheim.de

🚲 **Edeka G. Mannartz**, Spielesstr. 2, ☎ 2179, also E-Bike rental

Trittenheim lies on the inside of one of the characteristic bends of the Moselle and is home to the world renowned wine locations "Apotheke" and "Altärchen". From here, as his name would suggest, came the famous medieval scholar, abbot and humanist Johannes Trithemius (1462-1516) and the post war author, Stefan Andreas (1906-1970), was born in the valley of the "Kleinen Drohn", which lies in a forested area just south of the wine growing, Trittheim Mosel slopes. Well worth seeing, other than the impressive panorama, are an age-old Menhir (Standing

Moselle bend by Trittenheim

View over Piesport

stone), numerous wayside shrines, the ferry towers, the monument to Johannes Trithemius on the bridge arch as well as the church of St. Clemens and the chapel of St. Laurentius, located in the vinyards above the town.

Trittenheim to Bernkastel-Kues   28 km

Contune along the B 53 into Trittenheim ～ turn right into the **Brückenstraße** in the direction of Leiwen, which takes you towards the bridge over the Moselle ～ before the bridge turn right into a lane and ride down to the river bank ～ turn left ～ ride under the bridge and continue along the lane out of Trittenheim ～ follow the left bend after the sewerage treatment plant and the tennis courts

11 turn right onto the path beside the B 53 main road ~ continue on the bicycle path along the main road ~ turn right into a paved field road just before the bridge over the Moselle ~ ride under the bridge and follow the road along the river bank ~ pass the few houses of **Ferres** and continue until you reach the village of Piesport, which gives its name to the greater municipality of Piesport.

Piesport (Niederemmel)

Postal code: 54498; Area code: 06507

🛈 **Tourist Information**, Heinrich-Schmitt-Pl. 1, 📞 2027, www.piesport.de

🏛 **Roman wine press**, on the cycling route in the village of Piesport. The faithful reconstruction of a Roman wine press shows how Romans made their wine in the 3rd or 4th c. AD. It is housed within the well preserved remains of the original presshouse and cellars, discovered in 1985.

Aside from visiting the Roman wine press, which lies directly next to the bicycle route, it is also worth while taking a look at the baroque church of St. Michael. The village of Piesport also features a large number of charming little

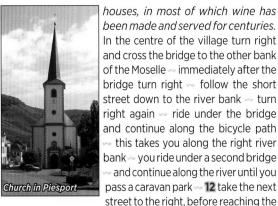
Church in Piesport

houses, in most of which wine has been made and served for centuries. In the centre of the village turn right and cross the bridge to the other bank of the Moselle ~ immediately after the bridge turn right ~ follow the short street down to the river bank ~ turn right again ~ ride under the bridge and continue along the bicycle path ~ this takes you along the right river bank ~ you ride under a second bridge ~ and continue along the river until you pass a caravan park ~ **12** take the next street to the right, before reaching the third bridge ~ at the main road turn left onto the bicycle lane ~ turn onto the bridge in the direction of Minheim and cross back to the left bank of the Moselle ~ after the bridge take the bicycle path to the left away from the main road ~ continue into the country lane and ride between the vinyards towards Minheim ~ keep left at the fork in the road by the first houses ~ and ride into Minheim.

Minheim

At the next intersection turn left, then immediately right, to take you into the **Moselwein-**

straße ~ continue along this street through the village ~ after the houses follow the right bend and cross the main road ~ turn left into a country lane immediately on the other side ~ follow the lane parallel to the main road ~ eventually you must cross the main road and continue to Kesten on the bicycle lane along the left side of the main road.

Kesten

As you reach Kesten keep leave the main road to the left beside the church and ride into the side street ~ at the T-intersection turn left ~ then turn right at the next street in the direction of Lieser and "Verkehrsbüro/Information" ~ simply follow this street out of Kesten and through the vinyards ~ at the T-intersection turn right ~ and right again at the next T-intersection where you reach the main road again ~ turn left here and ride on the bicycle lane along the left side of the main road towards Lieser and Bernkastel-Kues ~ you ride under a road bridge before crossing a bridge over the creek Lieser.

CONNECTION Just after the bridge you can connect with the Maare-Mosel cycling trail, which follows the Lieser upstream to the left.

Weinbaumuseum

Häferei

Noviand

Maring

Saar-Mosel bicycle trail

Osann

Lieser

Bernkastel-Kues

Lieser Palace

Wine museum
Cusanus Monastery

Museum of Local

Moselle

Bernkas

13

4,7

Monzel

Mülheim

Cusanus' birthplace

Landshut Castle

5,5

Brauneberg

Andel

Filzen

Kesten

Veldenzer Bach

Monzelfeld

Mühlheimer Wald

4,5

Veldenz

69

Wintrich

Thalveldenz

13 cross the road and ride into the paved path which takes you to the left along the bank of the Moselle ∼ you pass the town of Lieser.

Lieser

Postal code: 54470; Area code: 06531

- ℹ️ **Verhehrsbüro**, Am Markt 43, ✆ 8746
- 🏛️ Private local museum, Alois Heid, Hochstr. 8, ✆ 2777. Open by arrangement.
- 🏰 **Lieser Palace with palace gardens**, viewing by arrangement. Large residence in the Neo-Renaissance and Art Nouveau styles. Designed 1884-1887 by the architect Heinrich Theodor Schmidt for the winery owner and industrialist Eduard Puricelli and later extended (1895 and 1906) by Maria and Dr Clemens Freiherr von Schorlemer.
- ✳️ **Old postal station**, Am Alten Posthof 5, ✆ 94318. Former Thurn and Taxis postal station on the route from Brussels to Augsburg, Innsbruck and Italy. Founded in the 16th c.
- 🚴 **Verkehrsbüro**, Am Markt 43, ✆ 8746

Simply follow this paved path along the Moselle ∼ to the left is the L 47 ∼ you eventually reach a camping ground ∼ turn left at the T-intersection ∼ the street takes you to the right around a marina and back to the L 47 ∼ turn right onto the bicycle and pedestrian path ∼ and follow this path along the water to the bridge in Bernkastel-Kues **1**.

Bernkastel-Kues

TIP If you want to change to the other river bank in Bernkastel-Kues, turn left into the street **Nikolausufer** before reaching the bridge. At the intersection turn right into the **Saarallee** and ride to the roundabout, where you turn right again and cross the bridge.

Bernkastel-Kues

Postal code: 54470; Area code: 06531

- ℹ️ **Mosellandtouristik**, Kordelweg 1, Andel, ✆ 9733, www.mosellandtouristik.de
- ℹ️ **Mosel-Gäste-Zentrum** (Moselle Guest Centre), Gestade 6, Bernkastel, ✆ 500190
- ⚓ **Moselle river cruises: Hans Michels**, ✆ 8222, Bernkastel-Traben/Trarbach and back, departure 5x daily between 10 and 17, as well as sightseeing cruises. **Martin Kolb**, ✆ 4719, Bernkastel-Traben/Trarbach and back, departure 5x daily between 10 and 17.
- 🏛️ **Mosel Weinmuseum**, Cusanusstr. 2, ✆ 4141, Open: 16th Apr.-Oct., daily 10 - 17, guided tours and wine tasting, wine shop.
- 🏛️ **Cusanus birthplace**, Nikolausufer 49, ✆ 2831, Open: 16th Apr.-Oct., Tue-Sat 10-12 & 14:30-17, Sun 10-12. Exhibits about Nikolaus von Cues.
- 🏛️ **Heimatmuseum Graacher Tor (local museum)**, ✆ 7260, Open: Thur-Sun 15-17. City history exhibits in the only surviving city gate.
- 🏰 **St. Nikolaus Hospital (Cusanusstift)**, ✆ 2260, Tours by appointment. Medieval foundation with unique architecture, library with manuscripts by the scholar Nikolaus von Cues.
- 🏰 **Landshut Castle**, accessible by foot (30-45 minute walk)
- 🏊 **Moselbad**, Peter-Kremer-Weg, ✆ 3003 or 5019016
- 🚲 **Fun Bike Team "Die Bikeschmiede"**, Schanzstr. 22, ✆ 94024

The old city centre of Bernkastel deserves an unhurried visit. Start from the jewelbox-like market square. It is surrounded by stately old half-timbered houses, each of which merits a close inspection. The Rathaus, or city hall, which has grown bit by bit over the centuries, once housed the city's courts. The chains of the old pillory can still be seen hanging from the masonry. The coat of arms hangs between the arches of the glassed in arcade.

On the corner of the Römerstraße stands a house which was built in 1583. It has three tall stories above the low first floor, and carved animal heads decorate the window frames. The Spitzhäuschen in the Karlsstraße features similar decorations.

In the center of the square is the Michaelsbrunnen, a fountain built by Johann Ruprecht Hoffmann in 1606. A golden sword-wielding archangel stands on a squat pillar. The Graacher Straße leads to the Graacher Tor (Graach Gate), the only surviving part of the city's old defensive walls.

Bernkastel and the town of Kues on the opposite side of the river were united in 1905. Kues was the older of the two, in that a settlement dating back to the Neolithic period has been found there. The first written records to mention the wine and shipping town date from 1030.

A famous scholar from the waning middle ages came from Kues, and therefore took the name Nikolaus Cusanus. He studied law and natural sciences at the universities in Heidelberg and Padua, and later turned his attention to theology. He saw God as the combination of all opposites, and man as a microcosm of the infinite universe and divinity. He also studied political and church reforms, and the ideal of a single universal religion.

Finally, one anecdote about Bernkastel-Kues: When Beomund II, who lived in Burg Landshut, fell seriously ill with fever and his doctors were unable to help, one of his knights brought him a barrel of wine. After the prince had emptied the barrel, he recovered surprisingly fast. He therefore named the wine "Bernkastler Doctor," a name the vineyard still carries today.

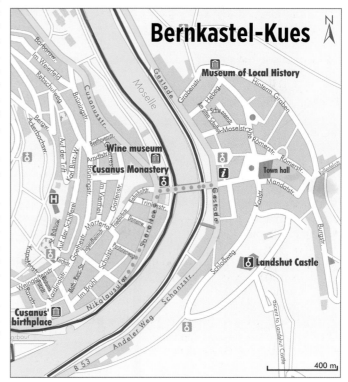

Trier to Bernkastel-Kues on the right bank

63 km

The route takes you out of Trier along the right bank of the Moselle. You can enjoy a ride through the Ruwer Valley along a former railway easement to the Sommerau castle ruin and the Riveris valley dam, or discover remains of the Roman settlements, such as the Villa Urbana in Longuich or the Villa Rustica in Mehring. Don't miss making a stop in Neumagen-Dhron, where a Roman fortification was unearthed. It is considered the oldest wine growing settlement in Germany, and a good place to sample some wine. Finally, the beautiful historic houses and romantic squares of Bernkastel-Kues are a crowning end to this section.

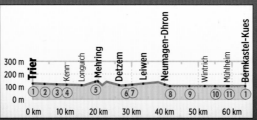

The route takes you along flat and paved bicycle paths and quiet streets throughout. Inclines are only to be found along the excursion into the Ruwer Valley.

The official main route of the Moselle river trail follows the left bank from Trier to Schweich and from there along the right bank.

72

Trier

Trier see page 43

Trier to Longuich   14.5 km

1 Start from the **Kaiser-Wilhelm-Brücke** and follow the paved bicycle path down the right bank of the Moselle ⌁ pass the river boat landings, the youth hostel and the outdoor pool ⌁ the path bends to the right after a large commercial building ⌁ turn right at the T-intersection ⌁ after a short distance turn left into the narrow path in front of the freeway bridge ⌁ follow the path through the underpass ⌁ after the underpass turn left ⌁ follow the street ⌁ **2** turn right at the next street, into **Rudolf-Diesel-Straße** ⌁ continue

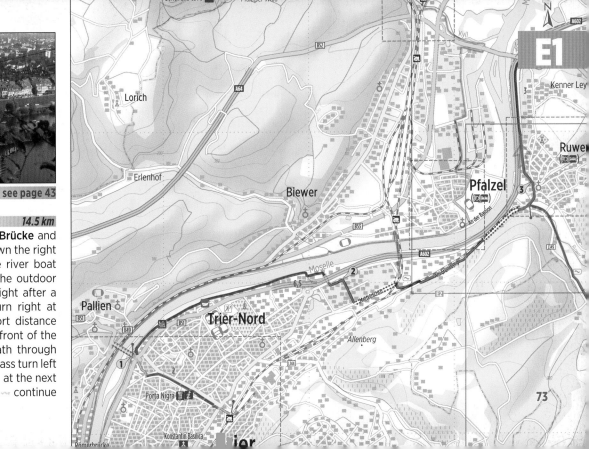

73

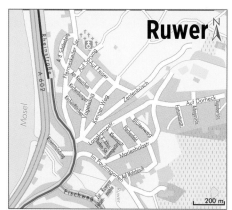

Ruwer N

to the T-intersection ∼ turn left onto **Metternichstraße** ∼ there are bicycle lanes on both sides ∼ as the street curves to the left, turn right and ride through the underpass below the railway tracks ∼ keep right after the underpass and follow the street ∼ cross the railway tracks ∼ turn left at the T-intersection onto the street **Am Grüneberg** ∼ you ride between forest and fields on one side and the railway tracks on the other ∼ continue straight onto the road ∼ a bicycle lane begins on the right hand side ∼ you pass a petrol station ∼ and ride into Ruwer.

Ruwer

EXCURSION The Ruwer-Hochwald Cycling Trail begins in Ruwer, along which you can make an excursion into the Ruwer Valley to Sommerau Ruin and the Riveris Dam.

Ruwer valley excursion   28 km

The Ruwer-Hochwald Cycling Trail makes for a comfortable ride, as it runs along the easement of the former Ruwer Railway. The Ruwer is a small tributary to the Moselle. Its source is in the Hunsrück, and the stream passes through rolling hills covered with extensive forests. This excursion takes you to the ruins of the Sommerau castle and the dam on the Riveris stream through quiet and idyllic surroundings. Pass the first side street ∼ turn right into a paved path after the left curve ∼ you are now on the easement of the former railway line and the start of the Ruwer-Hochwald Cycling Trail ∼ simply follow this path.

The sunny slopes of the Ruwer valley are also covered with vineyards. Most of these are Riesling vines, which have been cultivated in this area for centuries. The shaded hillsides are covered with forests that extend as far as the Saar-Hunsrück nature park.

You pass the edge of Metersdorf and soon after come to Kasel.

Kasel

Postal code: 54317; Area code: 0651

ℹ **Tourist Information Ruwer**, Bahnhofstr. 37a, ☎ 1701818, www. ruwer.eu

Monasteries in Trier operated profitable farm estates from Kasel. Those farms include the buildings that today form the "Kaseler Hof" inn. Its documented history goes back to 1373. Across the street from the inn is the "Marienkloster" estate, which once belonged to the St. Marien Monastery and is today in private hands.

Continue along the path past Kasel ∼ ride until you reach the former railway station at the edge of Waldrach.

Waldrach

🏛 **St.-Laurentius**, early Gothic parish church.

✳ **Keltermuseum (Wine making museum).** The German word "Keltern" derives from the latin word "calcare", which means "to tread with the feet," referring to the pressing of the fruit to extract the juice.

A section of the Roman aqueduct that brought the Ruwer's water to Trier since the 2nd century AD was discovered here. The city of Trier still draws its drinking water from the Ruwer to this day. After the former railway station the path crosses a bridge over the Ruwer and soon nears the main road.

Sommerau castle ruin

FORK Careful, this is where the routes to the Sommerau ruin and the Riveris dam diverge.

To Sommerau ruin

To reach the ruins of Sommerau castle, simply continue along the Ruwer-Hochwald Cycling Trail to Sommerau.

Sommerau

The ruins of Sommerau castle rise from the rocky hilltop like a giant broken tooth. On the inside of the rectangular tower one can still recognize parts of the castle's vaults, crenels and a chimney.

TIP If you have become interested in experiencing more of the Ruwer-Hochwald Cycling Trail, then there are another 39 km of wonderful cycling pleasure through Gusterath, Hentern, Kell am See and Reinsfeld to Hermeskeil awaiting you. More information under www.ruwer-hochwald-radweg.de

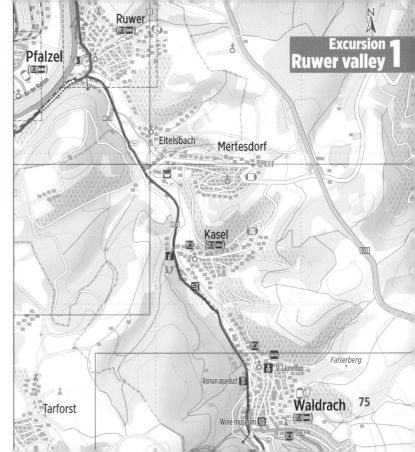

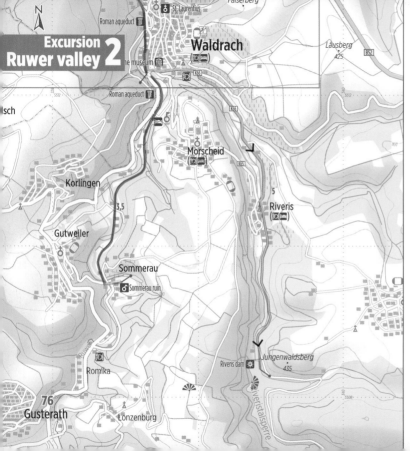

Waldrach

Lausberg
425

St. Laurentius

Roman aqueduct

ne museum

Roman aqueduct

Morscheid

Korlingen

5

Riveris

3,5

Gutweiler

Sommerau

Sommerau ruin

Romika

76
Gusterath

Lonzenburg

Jungenwaldsberg
435

Riveris dam

To the Riveris dam

Leave the bicycle path and turn right onto the main road ⌇ ride straight at the roundabout ⌇ pass the turnoff towards Morscheid ⌇ continue along the road ⌇ turn right into the side road in the direction of Riveris ⌇ the route takes you through the valley of the Riveris creek ⌇ you reach Riveris ⌇ turn left where the road makes a sharp right turn.

Riveris

Ride straight along the village street ⌇ after 1.5 km you reach a parking area ⌇ the road now climbs steeply to the top of the dam.

TIP If you have the time and desire, it is possible to walk the 8 km route around the reservoir. Swimming is naturally forbidden,

Riveris valley dam

as the reservoir provides drinking water for Trier and surrounding communities.

You return to the Moselle by the same route you arrived on ⌇ in Ruwer you once agin come to the Moselle River cycling route by the road ⌇ turn right and follow the main street through the town. To follow the main route simply continue along the main street through Ruwer ⌇ **3** keep left at the fork in the road ⌇ a bicycle path begins on the left hand side of the street just as you leave Ru-

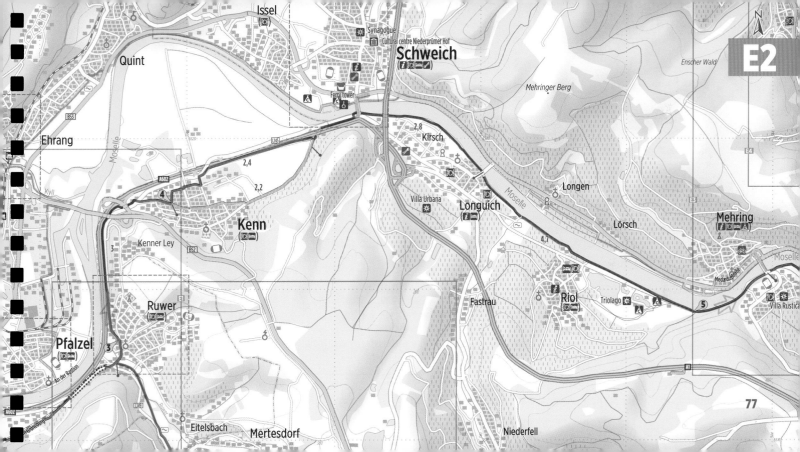

Issel

Quint

Schweich

Synagogue

Cultural centre Niederprümer Hof

Ferry Tower

Ehrang

Moselle

Kyll

Kirsch

2,8

2,4

2,2

Kenn

Kenner Ley

Villa Urbana

Longuich

Moselle

Longen

Lörsch

Mehring

Mehringer Berg

Enscher Wald

4,7

Fastrau

Riol

Triolago

Medardusmühle

Villa Rustica

Ruwer

Pfalzel

An der Bastion

Eitelsbach

Mertesdorf

Niederfell

Longuich, Villa Urbana

wer ~ follow the path as it takes you between the freeway and the L 145 ~ you pass under a large road bridge ~ as you reach the road turn left and follow the path under another road bridge ~ you ride into a commercial area at the edge of kenn.

Kenn

Take the first possible right turn ~ **4** turn into the second street to the left, **In der Ringebach** ~ turn right at the T-intersection ~ after 200 m turn left again, then immediately right ~ you ride through a commercial area ~ after the slight right bend in the road turn left into the lane ~ this takes you along the freeway for about 2 km, to your right the vine covered slopes rise beyond the fields ~ turn left at the T-intersection and ride on the bicycle path along the right side of the road ~ follow this under the freeway ~ keep right and ride directly underneath the freeway ~ the Moselle once again comes into view ~ before the first bridge cross the road and ride under the bridge ~ the path takes you along the river bank ~ you ride under the autobahn bridge ~ a paved road crosses the path just past the Autobahn bridge but you stay on the river bank ~ here you ride past a few orchards for a change, instead of the usual vineyards. As it happens, this community is called **Kirsch**, which is the German word for "cherry" ~ this hamlet almost merges with the next settlement, which is called Longuich.

Longuich

Postal code: 54340; Area code: 06502

🅸 **Tourist Information,** Maximinstr. 18, ✆ 1716, www.longuich-kirsch.de

✳ **Villa Urbana,** ruins and reconstructed parts of a Roman villa

🚲 **Mentchen,** Trierer Str. 35, ✆ 5804

The name Longuich is derived from the Celtic words "lunc" and "wich," which translate roughly as "crooked stream." This community belonged to the royal estate of Dezem and therefore also to St. Maximin abbey, which in the 13th century built a church in Longuich. Parts of this old church can still be seen in the current church.

The coat of arms above the gate of the big rectangular estate next door indicates this structure also dates back to the establishment of an abbey. The old castle stands about 200 m north of the church. Its massive gabled roof and quadratic slate foundation was occupied by the Benzerath family after the 16th century. A

The route by Mehring

chiseled stone image of Dorothea Benzerath can be found in the cemetery.

Longuich to Neumagen-Dhron 23.5 km
Small signs along the route serve as reminders that this was once the Roman wine road. The Romans transported their wine not only by boat, but by cart as well.

Follow the paved path along the bank of the Moselle, which is now dominated by vineyards as far as the eye can see ~ you pass the village of Riol.

Riol
Postal code: 54340; Area code: 06502

🛈 **Heimat- und Verkehrsverein Riol**, Hauptstr. 13, ✆ 995546, www.riol.de

✳ **Triolago recreational lake**, Zur Talstation 1, ✆ 937460. The 13 ha quarry pond is at the centre of an recreational area with boat hire, beach, lawns, summer toboggan run, restaurant and accommodation.

Continue along the river bank past the boat moorings and cam-ping ground ~ **5** the bicycle path comes to a road as you near the forest ~ you turn left and continue along the water to Mehring.

Mehring   see page 64
Ride straight ahead under the road bridge ~ keep left and follow the paved lane along the bank of the river ~ you pass a camping ground as you leave Mehring ~ you follow the Moselle past a forested area and vine covered slopes all the way to Detzem ~ just before the village you reach the turnoff to the locks, where you ride straight ahead into the bicycle path along the water.

Detzem
The tenth milestone, "ad decem lapidem," of the Roman road from Trier to Mainz gave the village of Detzem its name.

River barrages at regular intervals have helped make the river easier to control. These must be accompanied by locks, which allow

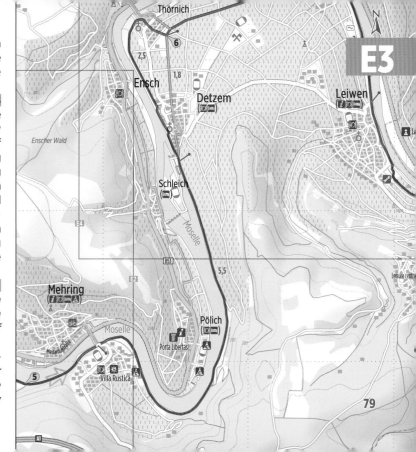

ships to pass the barrage and continue up, or down, the river. The cycle route leads past the locks at Detzem, where you can stop and watch the process of lifting or lowering a ship to the next level.

Continue past Detzem ∿ riding between the vinyards and the river you soon reach Thörnich ∿ at the intersection ride straight ahead into the **Moselstraße**.

Thörnich

Follow the right bend in the Moselstraße ∿ continue straight at the intersection with the **Hauptstraße** ∿ ride out of the village ∿ **6** turn left at a 4-way intersection in front of a building, where the streets cross at different angles ∿ follow the paved field road between the vinyards ∿ as you near Köwerich turn left at the 4-way intersection towards Bernkastel, Köwerich and the gasthaus "Alter Bahnhof" ∿ **7** turn right at the T-intersection ∿ follow this street, **Beethovenstraße**, into the centre of Köweich.

Köwerich

Turn left in the first street after the church ∿ ride through the underpass to reach the river bank, where you turn right and follow the bicycle path along the river ∿ you pass the town of Leiwen.

Leiwen

Postal code: 54340; Area code: 06507

🛈 **Tourist-Information Leiwen,** Römerstr. 1, ✆ 3100, www.leiwen.de

🚗 **Autohaus Wagner,** Auroniusstr. 15, ✆ 802010

Near the end of Leiwen you reach a road ∿ cross the road and continue on the bicycle path ∿ you pass a car parking area ∿ you come to ride on the former railway easement ∿ simply follow this elevated bicycle path ∿ by Trittenheim you pass below a road bridge ∿ cross the main road just after the old ferry tower and continue on the bicycle path along the right side of the main road **L 156** towards Neumagen-Dhron ∿ the route takes you between the vinyards for a short distance ∿ then back along the main road into Neumagen-Dhron

Neumagen-Dhron

Postal code: 54347; Area code: 06507

🛈 **Tourist-Information,** Hinterburg 8a, ✆ 6555, www.neumagen-dhron.de

🏛 **Heimatmuseum (local museum),** Hinterburg 8, ✆ 6555, Open: Mar.-Nov., Mon-Fri 8-12 & 14-17, Sat 10-12, Dec.-Feb., Mon-Fri 8-12.

🚗 **Radshop Kirsch,** Römerstr. 85, ✆ 939873

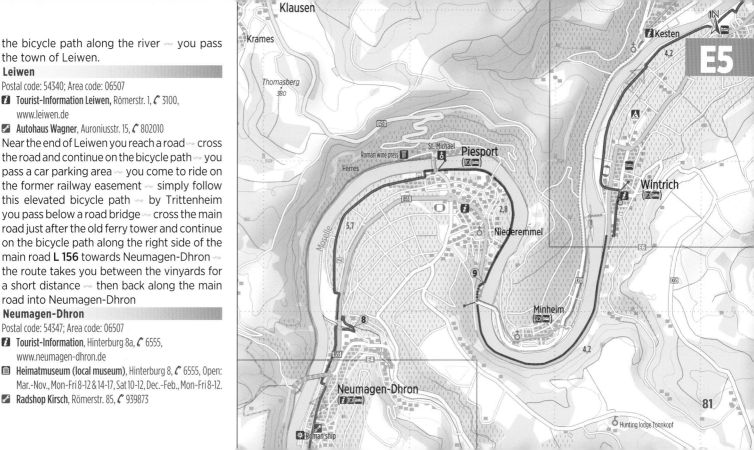

Neumagen can claim two honorary titles simultaneously. Not only is it "Germany's oldest wine town," it is also known as the "Pergamon of the Rhineland," a veritable paradise for archaeologists. When construction workers were digging to lay a new foundation, they stumbled on an old wall that was covered with reliefs. The local priest recognized that the walls were ancient and sold the decorated stones for one Mark per hundredweight, to the then recently-founded Rhineland State Museum in Trier.

Excavations at the site then produced a constant stream of new discoveries, new images and indeed entire series of images. No other site has provided as much information about the people who lived along the Moselle long ago. More than one thousand items delivered insights into local wildlife, winemaking and commerce, daily life and important festivals. Researchers later concluded that the walls belonged to an old Roman fort. Its outer walls formed the shape of an egg, and it had 14 towers and two gates. It was built at the command of Emperor Constantine I to defend the Trier to Mainz road from attacks by Germanic tribes. The most famous stone image shows a wine-

Bicycle path after Leiwen

ship and its happy helmsman. A concrete copy of the image can be seen along the village street. The originals are in the museum in Trier.

Neumagen-Dhron to Bernkastel-Kues   24.5 km

The route simply follows the main street into the town ~ before reaching the Moselle bridge, turn left just after the cemetery ~ turn right and ride below the bridge ~ follow the lane past a playing field and between the B 53 and vinyards ~ by the stream turn right a pass below the road bridge ~ continue to the small bridge, **8** where you cross the Dhronbach ~ follow the lane to the left back towards the B 53 and ride under the road bridge ~ follow the lane along the left side of the **B 53** for a

short distance ~ turn left and ride between the vinyards all the way to Niederemmel (Piesport) ~ turn left just after the cemetery and ride down to the Moselle ~ turn right and ride below the road bridge.

Piesport (Niederemmel)   see page 68

The Roman poet Ausonius praised the area around Piesport in his work "Mosella" from 361 BC. Archaeologists also made stunning discoveries at the edge of the world renowned wine growing slope "Piesporter Goldtröpfen". Not only was a Roman presshouse and cellar found, but also a rare diatret glass of the highest quality. Wealthy Romans in the 3rd century were often buried with these glasses. The name is derived from the Latin "diatretus," which translates roughly as "broken through." These glasses were made not by melting the glass, but by filling it to its shape.

Continue on the bicycle path along the river bank ~ you ride under another road bridge ~ ride along the river until you pass a caravan park ~ **9** take the next street to the right before the bridge ~ at the main road turn left onto the bicycle lane ~ which soon becomes a bicycle path ~ simply follow the bicycle path beside

Osann

Noviand

Maring

Lieser

Bernkastel-Kues

Graach-Schäfer

Lieser Palace

L47

Moselle

11

Wine museum
Cusanus Monastery

Museum of Local History

Monzel

Bernkastel

Cusanus' birthplace

Landshut Castle

Mülheim

5,5

Andel

Brauneberg

10

Monzelfeld

Kesten

4,2

B53

Filzen

E5

L158

Veldenzer Bach

Mühlheimer Wald

Veldenz

Wintrich

Thalveldenz

Burgen

the B 53 all the way to Wintrich ⌇ as you reach the first houses cross the bridge over the B 53 ⌇ turn left in the direction of Bernkastel-Kues and Brauneberg and ride along the street into the centre of the village.

Wintrich

Ride past the church ⌇ turn left at the next intersection into the **Moselstraße** ⌇ you once again cross a bridge over the B 53 ⌇ follow the right curve in the street ⌇ ride past the caravan parking area and a sports field ⌇ you ride along a paved lane between fields and vinyards ⌇ continue straight, offset to the left, at the intersection ⌇ **10** turn left at the intersection after a right bend in the lane ⌇ the houses of **Filzen** lie at a distance to your right ⌇ after another right bend in the lane turn sharply to the left at the 3-way intersection ⌇ you soon reach the edge of Brauneberg.

Brauneberg

Postal code: 54472; Area code: 06534

Niederemmel

ℹ **Tourist information**, Moselweinstr. 101, ☎ 933333, www.brauneberg.de

Simply follow the paved lane along the edge of the town ⌇ you soon ride along a bicycle path between fields again ⌇ the path then winds its way to the main road ⌇ where you continue on a bicycle path along the left side of the road ⌇ pass under the road bridge ⌇ to your right lies Mülheim.

Mülheim

Postal code: 54486; Area code: 06534

ℹ **Tourist Information**, Hauptstr. 60, ☎ 948734, www.muelheimmosel.de

Turn left away from the main road a short distance after the bridge ⌇ turn right by the river bank ⌇ follow the paved path along the river ⌇ follow the right curve ⌇ **11** at the T-intersection turn left ⌇ ride parallel to the main road for a short distance ⌇ at the next opportunity, just after the trees, turn left into the paved lane ⌇ you ride between fields and vinyards towards Andel.

Bernkastel-Kues

Andel

You reach a T-intersection the edge of Andel ⌇ turn left ⌇ then right by the water ⌇ you ride between the houses of Andel and the river ⌇ after a right bend you come back to the main road ⌇ turn left here onto the paved bicycle and pedestrian path ⌇ you leave Andel ⌇ the path takes you between the water and the B 53 all the way to Bernkastel-Kues ⌇ continue straight through the car parking area all the way to the **1** bridge over the Moselle.

Bernkastel-Kues see page 70

Bernkastel-Kues to Koblenz on the left bank

You now make your way from Bernkastel-Kues to Koblenz, the endpoint of the Moselle River Trail. Along the way there are numerous testaments to the age of the knights, such as the Marienburg on the ridge "Zeller Hamm", Arras Castle and Bischofstein Castle; an excursion takes you to the famous Eltz Castle in the fertile Maifeld. An additional highlight for those with a head for heights is the Calmont via ferrata, which winds its way along the top of the Calmont, Europe's steepest wine slope. Not just the taste, but the names invite you to sample wines such as the "Kröver Nacktarsch"! At the Deutschen Eck in Koblenz, where the Moselle flows into the Rhine, you have reached the end of the Moselle River Trail.

The route in this section takes you along flat and paved bicycle paths, bicycle lanes and quiet streets.

The main route follows the right bank as far as Zell, where it changes to the left bank and continue to Treis Karden before changing back to the right bank. In Alken the main route once again changes to the left bank, where it remains all the way to Koblenz.

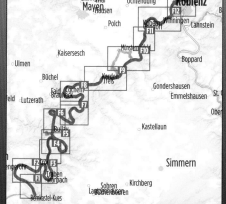

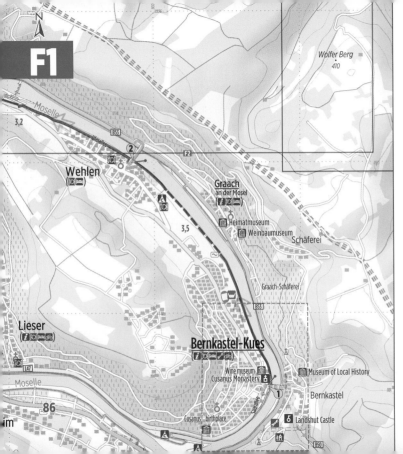

F1

Moselle

3,2

Wehlen

Moselle

Üferallee

B53

F2

Wolfer Berg
410

Graach
an der Mosel

Heimatmuseum

Weinbaumuseum

Schäferei

3,5

Graach-Schäferei

B53

Lieser

Bernkastel-Kues

Wine museum
Cusanus Monastery

Museum of Local History

Bernkastel

Saarallee

86

Cusanus' birthplace

Landshut Castle

B50

im

Bernkastel-Kues   see page 70

Bernkastel-Kues
to Traben-Trarbach   *21.5 km*

1 Ride under the road bridge and simply follow the paved path along the bank of the Moselle ⌇ you pass allotment gardens and the path becomes unpaved ⌇ the path is once again paved and you reach the first houses of Wehlen.

Wehlen

2 Ride straight ahead under the bridge along the **Uferallee** ⌇ continue straight ahead into the bicycle path out of Wehlen ⌇ follow the path to the left by the locks ⌇ continue on the bicycle lane along the main road ⌇ follow the bicycle path away from the road and under the bridge ⌇ the path changes to the left side of the road in front of Kloster Machern ⌇ follow the path along the main road all the way

Bernkastel-Kues

to Ürzig ⌇ just before the village the bicycle and pedestrian path changes to the right side of the road ⌇ continue with the traffic into the village.

Ürzig

By the car parking area turn left into a street which leaves the main road at an angle ⌇ continue to the right along the street **Moselufer** ⌇ at the intersection turn right ⤳ turn left just before the roundabout ⤳ continue along the quiet street Moselufer between the houses and the park ⤳ at the end of the street continue along the bicycle path and out of Ürzig ⤳ the path takes you along the left side of the main road towards Kinheim ⤳ **3** pass under a bridge ⤳ just before the houses of Kinheim you ride onto a lane parallel to the main road ⤳ keep left onto **Königsstraße**, which takes you into the centre of the village ⤳ keep left at the fork and ride straight ahead into the **Burgstraße**.

Kinheim

Postal code: 54538; Area code: 06532

ℹ Tourist Information, Moselweinstr. 14, ☎ 3444, www.kinheim.de

Turn right just after passing the church ⤳ turn left on the main road ⤳ a bicycle path begins on the left hand side just after the cemetery ⤳ you leave Kinheim and ride between vinyards ⤳ turn right where an gravel road continues straight and ride down to the main road ⤳ turn left onto the bicycle path, which takes you along the left side of the road into Kröv.

Kröv

Postal code: 54536; Area code: 06541

ℹ️ Tourist Information Kröv, Moselweinstr. 35, ✆ 9486, www.kroev.de

✉️ Outdoor pool, Moselweinstr., ✆ 9653

The "Kröver Nacktarsch" vineyard and its wines have helped Kröv become known among wine-lovers around the world. No wonder, when one considers the stories concerning the curious name of the wine, which means "bare bottom." According to one version, the name was invented in the 1920s by a couple of wags from the village, and quickly became popular in the region, in part because it was known that the 16th century knight Götz von Berlichingen allegedly liked the wine. Another legend is that monks from the monastery at Wolf planted grape vines on a bald hillock and were pleased to discover this "naked bottom" delivered a good and bountiful harvest.

Yet another story is even more graphic. It claims that the estate in Kröv gave the vinyard workers one day on which they could harvest grapes for their own use. The workers labored especially hard

Moselle by Traben-Trarbach

that day, which proved expensive for the local governor. So he ordered a pig to be slaughtered and served to his workers in the morning of the day they were to harvest grapes for themselves. The greasy, fresh meat gave the workers horrible diarrhea, which slowed their work. But one man refused to let his discomfort stop him from collecting grapes. Instead, he took of his trousers and continued to work while he emptied his bowels. When the governor saw this, he allegedly said, "I've been outsmarted by someone with a bare bottom!"

After the bicycle path stops continue through Kröv on the bicycle lane ∽ at the end of the town a bicycle path begins on the left hand side once more ∽ you ride beside the main road all the way to the Moselle bridge leading to Wolf ∽ here you continue straight and ride under the bridge ∽ from here you must ride with the traffic on the main road towards Rißbach.

Rißbach

Ride through the small village ∽ **4** turn right into the paved path just after the camping ground ∽ the path winds its way to the river bank and takes you along the river into Traben-Trarbach ∽ you pass a playing field ∽ continue between the houses and the river ∽ you reach the bridge which connects Traben with Trarbach across the Moselle.

Traben-Trarbach

Postal code: 56841; Area code: 06541

ℹ️ Tourist Information, Am Bahnhof 5, ✆ 83980, www.traben-trarbach.de

🚢 Moselle passenger ships, Gebr. Kolb, scheduled service to Bernkastel and Cochem, ✆ 02673/1515.

🏛️ Mittelmosel-Museum, In the Baroque villa Haus Böcking, Casinostr. 2, ✆ 9480, Open: Easter-Oct., Tue-Sun 10-17. Presents residential culture of the 18th and 19th c. as well as the history of town.

🏛️ Fahrrad Museum (Bicycle Museum), Moselstr. 2, ✆ 5905, Open: Tue-Fri 11-13 & 14-18, Sat, Sun 11-13. Displays bicycles from the beginning to the present. Free entry.

Haus der Ikonen (Icon Museum), Trarbach, Mittelstr. 8, ✆ 812408, Open: Palm Sunday to 1 Nov., Tue–Sun 10–17, Low season, Sat, Sun/ Hol. 10–17. Displays the collection of the deceased iconograph Alexej Saweljew.

Buddha museum, Bruno Möhring Pl. 1, ✆ 8165180, Open: Tue–Sun 10–18. Entry fee: € 15. Permanent exhibition of more than 1000 Buddha sculptures.

Mont Royal, excavations of a French fortress (built 1680–1697 by Louis XIV). Guided tours can be arranged at the tourist information centre.

Grevenburg Ruin, built 1350–57. The Sponheimers governed the "count's rear country" from this castle until 1437. They were followed by 13 different owners before the French finally destroyed the castle in 1735. Today there is a restaurant in the ruins of the castle.

Historic gate tower. Part of the medieval town defences, which today serves as viewing tower. Glockenspiel.

Mosel Adventure Forest, Mont Royal, ✆ 817772, Open: May–Sept. daily 10–20, Oct., 10–18. The park has several climbing parcours and a climbing wall.

Egon Wagner, Brückenstr. 42, Trarbach, ✆ 1649

Nestled between the characteristic Moselle landscape of vinyards and forests lies the architectural jewel of Traben-Trarbach. About one hundred years ago, at the turn of the century, the city's wine merchants built a number of fine art nouveau buildings. The architects at work included Professor Bruno Möhring of Berlin. Their creations have been carefully maintained and preserved to this day. Not just art nouveau, but the entire range of "Belle Epoque" splendor was attracted to Traben-Trarbach, making the city a favorite destination for lovers of the baroque and classical styles. The spa at Bad Wildstein offers an excellent place to soothe tired muscles, in

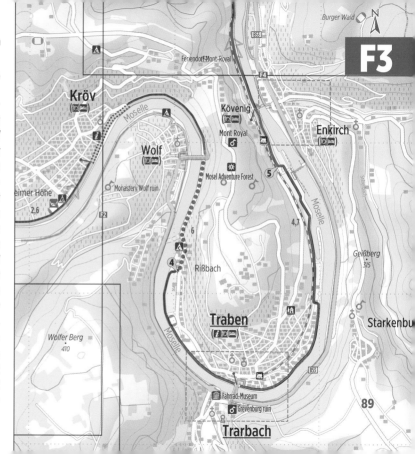

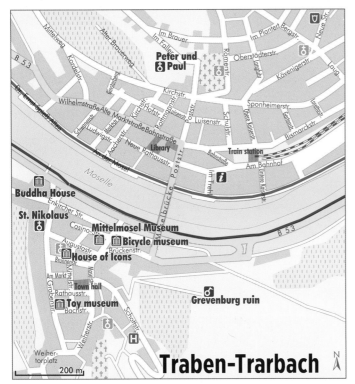

Traben-Trarbach

Peter und Paul

Buddha House
St. Nikolaus
Mittelmosel Museum
Bicycle museum
House of Icons
Town hall
Toy museum
Library
Train station
Grevenburg ruin

B 53

Moselle

200 m

N

the hot baths of the "Moseltherme." Wine connoisseurs, or just visitors who wish to learn more about the Moselle's fine wines, can follow the "Traben-Trarbacher Riesling Route" from wine cellar to wine cellar.

Traben-Trarbach to Kaimt   19 km

Ride under the bridge and continue beside the river ~ the path eventually turns away from the river by the last houses ~ turn right in the direction of Kövenig at the T-intersection ~ you ride parallel to the railway tracks, which are above to the left ~ continue past the marina ~ the bicycle path briefly takes you back out to the Moselle, then straight ahead past the lock ~ straight past the

buildings ~ follow the street to the left to a T-intersection ~ **5** turn right and ride along the street into Kövenig.

Kövenig

Postal code: 54536; Area code: 06541

🛈 **Tourist Information Kröv**, ☎ 9486, www.kroev.de

⛴ **Passanger ferry to Enkirch**. Operates: Apr. - Oct., Mon-Sat 9-12 & 13-18:30, Sun/Hol 9-12 & 14-18 and by arrangement under ☎ 6895 or 3740

Simply follow the street between the Moselle and the railway line

Near Reil

out of the village ～ continue to Reil.

Reil

Postal code: 56861; Area code: 06542

ℹ️ Tourist Information Reil, Hutg. 16, ✆ 21036, www.reil-mosel.de

Continue along the street between the Moselle and the houses of Reil ～ **6** you pass under the bridge ～ continue straight ahead on the quiet rural lane out of Reil ～ you come to ride between the river and steep vinyards ～ the railway line on the slope above runs along an arched viaduct before entering an tunnel ～ after rounding the river bend you eventually pass a ferry landing.

TIP Here you have the chance to take a ferry to Pünderich on the other bank of the river. ✆ 06542/900021 for information concerning ferry operating times.

Marienburg

Simply continue along the asphalt lane ～ **7** you soon reach a fork.

EXCURSION By turning left here you have the opportunity to shorten your route considerably by cutting across the "Zeller Hamm" to the B 53, where you turn left to join the main route on the bicycle lane. You can also make an excursion to the nearby Marienburg or the lookout tower on the Prinzenkopf.

To continue along the main route, turn right and ride along the river for a short distance ～ turn left into

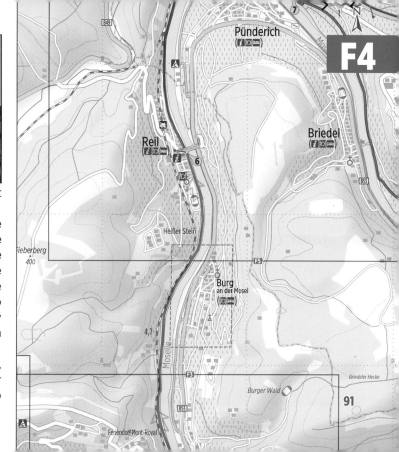

F4

91

the first side lane ～ it makes a right bend and takes you between vinyards ～ continue straight into the paved lane at the 5-way intersection ～ follow this lane back to the river and along the river bank.

The "Zeller Hamm"

Between Pünderich and Bullay the Moselle curves through the Zeller Hamm, a long tight loop which doubles back on itself. The word "Hamm" refers to the part of a horse harness which is placed around the neck of the animal. The narrowest part of the ridge between the two parts of the river is crowned by the Marienburg, from which you can see the river down both sides. The unique location made it

Marienburg

popular through the millennia. First the Celts had a ceremonial site on the mountain, and then the Romans built a fortress there. Later it was the site of a Frankish king's estate, then an archbishop's castle, and the Peterskirche. In 1156 the castle was turned into a convent for Augustine nuns. In 1515 Count Richard von Greiffenklau closed the convent under the pretext that the nuns were not obeying the strict rules of their order. He then rebuilt the fortifications. The battles and sieges of the Thirty Years War caused extensive damage, and in 1687 the French destroyed the fortification. After extensive rennovations it now houses an educational facility.

You reach a fork in the road by a ferry landing ～ continue straight along the river bank.

TIP From here you can take a ferry to Briedel on the other river bank. ✆ 06542/4640 or 06542/4013 for information concerning ferry operating times.

Follow the paved lane as it leaves the river ～ you ride between vinyards until you reach a T-intersection on the bend of a street ～ turn

Bick in die Weinberge bei Barl/Kaimt

right and follow the street back to the river ～ **8** turn left at the T-intersection by the river bank ～ you ride under a bridge ～ follow the street along the river ～ the town of Kaimt lies to your left.

Kaimt

Kaimt to Ediger-Eller   15 km

Continue along the river ～ turn left just before the pedestrian bridge into the street **Marienthaler Au** ～ follow this street all the way up to the main road ～ ride onto the bicycle path along the right side of the main road ～ you pass under the upper deck of a double-decker bridge ～ continue into Alf.

Alf

Postal code: 56859; Area code: 06542

ℹ️ **Tourist Information,** Ferdinand-Remy-Str. 11, 📞 2619 or 2419, www.alf-mosel.de

🏛️ **Village Museum,** Auf Kockert 10, 📞 2619 or 2671, Open: May - Oct., Sat 16-18. Free entry.

✉️ **Outdoor pool Arrestal,** 📞 22970.

Continue along the bicycle path beside the main road ∾ at the roundabout continue straight.

EXCURSION The historic centre of Alf lies to the left of the roundabout and from here you can also make an excursion to Arras castle.

Excursion to Arras Castle

At the roundabout take the second exit and turn right into the **Brückenstraße**, which takes you into the historic town centre ∾ turn left into the **Ferdinand-Remy-Straße**, which later becomes the **Mühlenstraße** ∾ turn right when you reach the main road ∾ a bicycle lane runs along the left side ∾ follow the road until you reach a turnoff to Burg Arras to the left ∾ you ride across a bridge and ascend to the castle.

Arras Castle

🏛 **Castle Museum**, ✆ 22275, Open: Mar.-Dec., daily 10-18.

The castle stands on a 200 m rock, and the road up is steep. But the view from the comfortable restaurant is spectacular and well worth the effort. Another local legend describes how the castle came into being:

After a giant smithy and his twelve equally large sons managed to stop the Huns from reaching the Eifel highlands from the Moselle, the emperor Otto I knighted the brave man in 938 and gave him the fortress as a fiefdom. Today the castle is a hotel and restaurant, and has an interesting museum with exhibits about the history of the Moselle river valley. Other attractions include the keep, the inner courtyard, the banquet hall and the dungeon.

After the roundabout you continue along the bicycle path ⁓ after a short distance a bicycle and pedestrian path leads to the right, away from the road and along the river bank ⁓ simply follow this paved path to St. Aldegund.

St. Aldegund

You ride along the river, the houses of the village to your left ⁓ after crossing a small bridge the path once again follows the main road out of the village ⁓ simply follow the bicycle path along the right side of the B 49 **9** you pass under a bridge ⁓ a short distance after the bridge turn right into the paved lane ⁓ you ride btween the road and the river past small garden plots towards Bremm ⁓ the lane takes you back to the main road beside the centre of Bremm.

Bremm

Bremm is a charming little wine village with narrow streets. It lies at the foot of the Calmont, whose slopes of 65 to 76 percent make its vinyards Europe's steepest.

EXCURSION Between Bremm and Eller you may want to try the "Calmont Klettersteig", which is a via ferrata along the vinyards and cliffs of the Calmont. Start and end points are in Bremm above the church and in Ediger-Eller at the railway bridge. An hourly bus service runs between the two communities for the return trip.

Calmont Klettersteig

The via ferrata, completed in 2001, lies at the heart of a network of hiking trails which connect the communities of Bremm, Ediger-Eller and Neef. This narrow hiking trail takes you through Europe's steepest vinyards along a 3 km long route, which is secured with 6 ladders, about 100 safety ropes, 22 stirrups and 16 spikes to make it passable. The trip is undertaken under your own responsibility and requires good foot-wear, good weather, reasonable physical fittness and a head for heights. Children must be super-vised at all times. Duration is about 2-3 hours.

At the main road in Bremm turn right and followthe bicycle path along the right side of the main road ⁓ you leave Bremm and round a bend in the river. To your left rise Europe's steepest vinyards on the slopes of the Calmont and the ruins of Stuben Monastery can be seen across the river.

The path leaves the road and follows the river bank as you pass below the railway bridge ⁓ you cross the Ellerbach ⁓ to your left lie the houses of Eller ∿ continue along the bicycle path to Ediger.

Ediger-Eller

Postal code: 56814; Area code:02675

ℹ **Tourist Information Ediger-Eller**, Ediger, Pelzerstr. 1, ✆ 1344, www.ediger-eller.de

⛪ **St. Martius church** (15th c.), Ediger. The church not only boasts impressive stellar vaulting and a richly furnished interior, but has what is considered to be the most beautiful gothic tower on the Moselle, with a majestic peal of bells, second only to that of the Cathedral of Trier.

Eller and Ediger, which joined together administratively in 1969, both belonged to the realm of the Frankish king Dagobert I and therefore share a common history much longer than the last few decades. One especially noteworthy house in Eller is the Zehnthaus to which more than 70 villages brought their tithes, one-tenth of their harvest, which the provost of Trier collected.

Ediger has retained much of its historic character, thanks to intensive restoration and care of its oldest buildings. More than 60 houses date from the 16th and 17th centuries, plus 7 houses from the 18th century and a large number from the 19th century combine to form a delightful ensemble of structures. Ediger forms a prime example of the typical river village found along the Moselle. One main street runs parallel to the shoreline, and is crossed by many short alleys that run down to the river.

Two things that have been especially important to the people of the Moselle over the centuries are their faith, and the wine. Just how important, and how inter-linked, faith and wine are can be seen in a painted relief in a rather simple chapel in the vineyard above the town. The image, "Christ and the

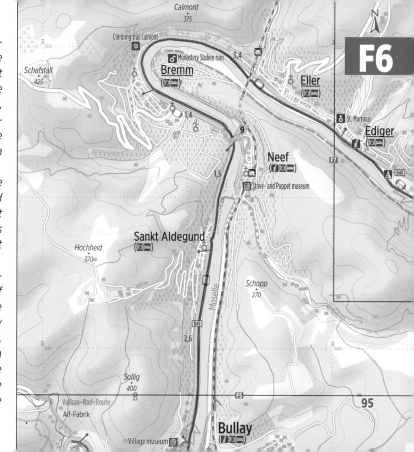

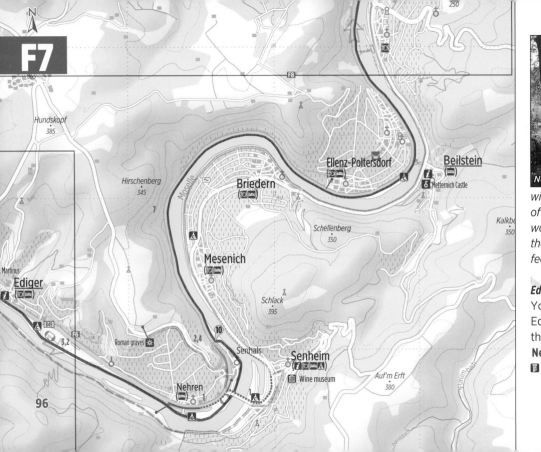

N

Hundskopf
385

Hirschenberg
345

Moselle

7

Briedern

Ellenz-Poltersdorf

Beilstein

Metternich Castle

Schellenberg
350

Kalkbe
350

Martinus
Ediger

Mesenich

B49

F6
3,2

Roman graves

10

2,4

Senhals

Schlack
395

Senheim

Wine museum

Auf'm Erft
380

Nehren

250

F8

Near Nehren

wine press," illustrates the wine-blood symbolism of the church. A spindle presses blood from the wounds of the body of Christ, as he suffers under the weight of his cross, while at the same time his feet stomp the grapes in the wine press trough.

Ediger-Eller to Cochem   21 km

You pass a camping ground as you leave Ediger-Eller ∿ follow the bicycle path along the river to Nehren.

Nehren

Roman Graves. In the vinyards above Nehren lie burial chambers from the 3rd to 4th c. AD. The original wall paintings in the two chambers are the best preserved vault paintings of their kind north of the alps. The upper part of the monuments have been reconstructed.

EXCURSION If you want to visit the Roman graves or cross the river to Senheim, turn left before the water body by the camping ground and follow the route indicated on map F7.

Continue on the path along the river past the camping ground ～ you pass under the road bridge leading to Senheim on the opposite bank ～ continue along the bicycle path and you soon reach **Senhals** ～ continue on the street where the path ends ～ follow the left curve to the main road **10** here you turn right onto the bicycle path ～ follow the path along the main road all the way to Poltersdorf.

Poltersdorf

⛴ **Ferry to Beilstein,** ☎ 02673/1515

Continue on the bicycle path along the main road past Poltersdorf ～ you pass the ferry landing and reach Ellenz shortly afterwards.

Ellenz

Continue on the bicycle path along the main road past Ellenz ～ you pass a barrage on the Moselle ～ after passing under a bridge, turn

right into the bicycle path ~ this takes you parallel to the main road towards Ernst.

Ernst

Postal code: 56814; Area code: 02671

- 🚲 **Bioladen "Wilder Wein"**, Moselstr. 45, ✆ 5551, www.bioladen-wilder-wein.de

You ride along the edge of the village ~ after passing the houses of Ernst the bicycle path once more comes to follow the main road ~ you pass to the right of the Franciscan **Ebernach Monastery**, which today serves as a home for intellectually disabled persons ~ ride along the promenade past Sehl.

Sehl

- 🚲 **Radsport Schrauth**, Sehler Anlagen 10, ✆ 02671/7974

Continue on the bicycle path along the main road and you soon reach Cochem.

Cochem

Postal code: 56812; Area code: 02671

- ℹ️ **Tourist Information Ferienland Cochem**, Endertpl. 1, ✆ 60040, www.ferienland-cochem.de
- ⚓ **Moselle passenger ships**, Gebr. Kolb OHG, ✆ 02673/1515. Scheduled departures to Traben-Trarbach, Zell and Beilstein as well as sightseeing tours.

- 🏰 **Reichsburg Cochem**, ✆ 255. Construction of the castle was begun in the year 1000 by the Palatinate counts.
- ☀ **Chair-lift to the Pinnerkreuz**, ✆ 989063, Open: Easter - mid Nov. Excellent views of the city and the Moselle river valley.
- ☀ **Historic Mustard Mill**, ✆ 607665, open all year.
- 🦌 **Wildpark Klotten (Game park)**, ✆ 7660, a game park above the Cochem train station, can be reached by foot from the top station of the chair-lift.
- 🏊 **Recreational centre Moselbad**, ✆ 97990, Indoor pool, wave pool, children's water park, sauna and solarium.
- 🚲 **Schaltwerk**, Ravenéstr. 18-20, ✆ 603500
- 🚲 **Fahrrad-Shop Hans Werner Kreutz**, Endertstr. 35, ✆ 91131 or 91138
- 🚲 **KD-Agentur**, Moselpromenade, ✆ 4610

Evening in Cochem

Cochem has been a popular tourism destination since the 19th century. Today the city hosts about 2.5 million day-time visitors and 500,000 overnight stays per year, far outstripping all other Moselle river localities. A total of 150 hotels and restaurants serve the visitors. In addition to the many recreational facilities, the beautifully preserved old town and the castle are powerful tourism magnets.

The earliest known reference to the city dates back to the year 886, with a mention of a settlement named Cochuma. A castrum Cuochomo was first named in the year 1051. This castle was one of the properties belonging to the Polish queen Richeza, a daughter of Emperor Otto III. She bequeathed the castle to her cousin under the condition that he protect the Brauweiler abbey, which her parents had established. When the Archbishop Anno von Köln attacked the properties, the cousin was defeated and had to spend 3 years imprisoned in the Gorze monastery in Lorraine. Upon his release, he returned and in his madness murdered his wife. Violent disputes over the property continued in the years that followed.

Moselpromenade in Cochem

Emperor Konrad III seized the castle as a fief, and in 1294 King Adolf von Nassau pledged it to the Archbishop Beomund von Trier, and Cochem came under the control of Trier. Archbishop Balduin blocked the river with a heavy chain and demanded tolls from the ships that plied the river. The revenues enabled him to expand the castle and improve the city's defenses. Unlike many other cities along the Moselle, Cochem survived the Thirty Years War in relatively good shape, but then suffered extensive damage at the hands of the French during the war of the Palatinate Succession. The Berlin financier Ravené acquired the castle and rebuilt it between 1868-77 as his summer residence. Today the castle is open to the public.

Cochem to Hatzenport   22.5 km

Pass under the bridge ⁓ ride onto the bicycle and pedestrian path which runs along the right side of the street ⁓ follow the path out of Cochem ⁓ **11** you pass under another bridge ⁓ follow the bicycle lane beside the main road **B 49** to Klotten ⁓ as you reach the town continue along the bicycle path between the road and the river.

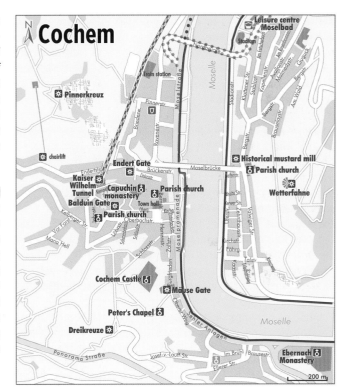

Klotten

- **Ferry across the Moselle**. Operates: Good Friday-5th Jul., Sat, Sun/Hol 10-17, 6th Jul.-22nd Sept., daily 10-13 & 14-18, 23rd Sept.-Oct., daily 10-12 & 14-17
- **Coraidelstein castle ruin**. Begun in 960, the castle went through many hands and was in use until the early 19th c., after which it fell into ruin.

The ruins of the Coraidelstein castle throne the bluff above the small town of Klotten. The first stone is said to have been laid by Count Hermann I of the Palatinate, in the 10th century. The effort of climbing up to the ruins is compensated by the excellent views across the landscape. Vineyards no longer dominate the view. Klotten's prosperity was derived in part from the slate that was quarried nearby for railroad construction. The stone was loaded in Klotten, making the village an important landing for the river's shipping.

The houses of Klotten lie to your left ～ you pass the ferry landing ～ as you leave Klotten, the bicycle path once more follows the main road ～ continue to Pommern ～ you pass a camping ground as you reach the village.

Pommern

Postal code: 56829; Area code: 02672

- **Tourist-Information Treis-Karden**, Hauptstr. 27, Treis, ✆ 6137, www.treis-karden.de
- **Martberg Archaeological Park**, on the Martberg between Pommern and Karden. Open: May-Oct., Fri-Sun 11-17. A free shuttle bus from the centre of Pommern is available on weekends and holidays on request, ✆ 910133.

You once more follow a bicycle lane along the main road B 49 ～ as you reach Treis-Karden, follow the bicycle path to the right and **12** under the bridge which connects Trais and Karden.

> **TIP** The official main route changes to the right bank of the Moselle in Treis-Karden. You will find the corresponding route description on page 129.

Treis-Karden

Postal code: 56253; Area code: 02672

- **Tourist-Information**, St.-Castor-Str. 87, ✆ 9157700, www.treis-karden.de
- **Moselle passenger ships**, Köln Düsseldorfer, ✆ 1697 or 0221/2088-318 . Service to Koblenz: 14th Jun.-6th Oct., Fri.-Sun. Also take bicycles.

- **Moselle passenger ships**, Gebr. Kolb OHG, ✆ 02673/1515 or 0172/4715374. Daily river cruises as well as a service to Koblenz every Friday. Also take bicycles.
- **Stiftsmuseum (Collegiate Museum)**, St. Castor-Str., next to the church, Karden, Open: Easter & May-Oct., Fri 14-17, Sat, Sun/hol., 10-12 & 14-17. Rich collection detailing 2000 years of local hisotry.
- **Collegiate church St. Castor**, Lindenplatz, Karden, Open: May-Oct., daily 11-17. Architecturally noteworthy church with Stumm organ (1728), terracotta altar (1420) and Gothic wall paintings dating from 1495.

Kastor, a pupil of the Trier Bishop Maximin, and his companions Pontentius, Felicius and Simplicius founded a Christian community in the settlement of Cardena. After their deaths, they were honored as saints and the town grew in significance.

In the Frankish period Karden was the centre of a broader pastoral district, and the priests lived together as a community. This community eventually became the St. Kastor seminary. It included a school which was decorated with elaborate wall paintings. In 1951 two fresco series were exposed, showing Susanne from the Apocrypha of the bible, and the saga of

Binningen

Kail

Brieden

Eichenberg
270

Pommern

Kesselkopf
280

Karden

Monastery museum

St. Castor

Pommerer Mart
270

Archäologiepark Martberg

Fahrlei
265

Zilleskapelle

Treis

Pilliger Heck

Eltz Castle

Ringelsteiner Mühle

Müdenerberg

Klickerterhof

Dömpel
270

Müden

Moselle

Traiser Berg
470

Schock
425

Lütz

Moselkern

Henry the Lion, who made a pilgrimage to the Holy Land.

Continue along the bicycle lane, which now follows the **B 416** out of Treis-Karden to Müden.

Müden

Simply continue on the bicycle lane along the main road B 416 past Müden ∿ you soon reach Moselkern.

Moselkern

⚓ **Moselle passenger ships,** Köln Düsseldorfer, ✆ 02671/980023 or 0221/2088-318 . Service to Koblenz: 14th Jun.-6th Oct., Fri-Sun. Also take bicycles.

⚓ **Moselle passenger ships,** Gebr. Kolb OHG, ✆ 02673/1515 or 0172/4715374. Daily river cruises as well as a service to Koblenz every Friday. Also take bicycles.

ALTERNATIVE From here you can visit Eltz Castle, possibly the most beautiful castle by the Moselle, and begin the inland route via Münstermaifeld to Hatzenport. The trip to the castle is not easy, however, as it can only be reached from this side over a foot path, with over 100 steps.

Moselkern

To Eltz Castle and Münstermaifeld   17.5 km

This excursion takes you along the Eltzbach to the impressive Eltz Castle and on to Münstermaifeld, where long climbs cannot be avoided as you ride up into the fertile Maifeld region. Then you pass a series of mills as the road winds back down the romantic Schrumpf valley towards Hatzenport on the Moselle.

Just before entering Moselkern, turn left into the side road just in front of the camping ground ∿ at the T-intersection turn right ∿ you ride over a little stream, the Eltzbach ∿ turn left opposite the car parking area into the **Kirchstraße** ∿ turn

left in front of the church ∿ then follow the right bend and ride under the railway tracks, keeping an eye open for signs to Burg Eltz ∿ the road passes through the Eltz valley for 2 km to the Mühlengasthaus ∿ the footpath up the castle starts from the large parking area.

TIP You can park your bicycle at the parking lot, which has an attendant. However, because you can continue from the castle onward to Münstermaifeld and the Schrumpf valley, you may wish to consider pushing your bicycle up the 2 km path. Be forewarned, one part of the walk is quite steep! It is not recommended to those carrying baggage.

Eltz Castle

⚔ Eltz Castle, ✆ 02672/950500, Open: 24th Mar.-3rd Nov., daily 9:30-17:30. The castle has remained in the same family since its construction and sustained no war damage. This has allowed its original architecture and interiors from over 8 centiuries to survive. Displays of medieval furnishings and weapons as well as a treasure chamber containing valuable items of gold and silver, coins, jewelry, glass and porcelain.

Eltz Castle stands on a steep crag of rock in the narrow Eltz valley, surrounded by deep green

Naunheim

Mörz

Mersberg
215

Bleidenberg

Kattenes

Wallfa

St. Martin und Severus

Local History Museum

Münstermaifeld

Metternich

3,5

Thurant-Castle

Alken

Schafberg
370

Sevenich

2,8

Kergeshöfe

Schromber Thalsberg
3,4

Probstmühle

Löf

Schrumpftal

2,8

Wildenbunge
350

Antoniuskapelle

Wierschem

Hatzenport

0.6

St. Johannis

Ferry Tower

Moselle

Brodenbach

Keldung

Rothenberg
270

Donnerloch

Langer Berg
295

Werth

Lasserg

Moselle

Pfarrbüsch
235

Jährsberg
295

Jahrsberger Höfe

5,5

B416

3

Tholeisterhof

F9

Bischofstein Castle

Burgen

Ehrenburg

Elzbach

Eltz Castle

Moselle

Höber Berg
300

Kröpp

405

Moselle

B49

B416

K41

K40

L207

B49

L206

woods that come right up to the castle's walls. The castle itself is composed of many towers, battlements, bay-windows, porches and roofs along and on top of the tall old walls. It does not take much fantasy to imagine one self transported into a world in which knights defended the countryside and roads from impregnable mountaintop fortresses like Burg Eltz.

Eltz castle

In the 13th century the family that owned Eltz divided into several different lines, each of which occupied its own house. Because the fortress offered only limited space, the castle grew in height as various wings and courtyards were added to an increasingly complicated assemblage of walls and spaces.

ALTERNATIVE After the tour of the castle, either return to Moselkern the way you came or, if you brought your bicycle this far, set off on the alternative route over Münstermaifeld.

From the start you need to work really hard, you may even have to push the bicycle up the extremely steep paved road that leads from the castle bridge up to the right ⇝ you soon come to a parking lot, from which you reach the somewhat wider road to Wierschem ⇝ another smaller climb follows, so you may be ready for a short rest by the time you reach Wierschem.

Wierschem

You can cool off at the village fountain ⇝ follow the main street through the village ⇝ continue up one last hill as you leave Wierschem ⇝ soon the road brings you to Münstermaifeld ⇝ turn left at the T-intersection into **Obertorstraße** ⇝ as you reach a square turn right into the **Martinstraße** ⇝ this brings you directly onto the **Münsterplatz**.

Münstermaifeld

Postal code: 56294; Area code: 02605

Heimatmuseum, old Propstei, ✆ 3556, Open: Apr.-Oct., Wed-Sat 14-17. The museum displays an original bakery, hairdresser, tobacco shop, shoemaker's workshop and classroom.

Former collegiate church of St. Martin and St. Severus. Münsterplatz. First begun around 573-596 on the foundations of a Roman watch tower. Present day building mostly from the 12th to 14th c. Frescos from the 13th to 15th c.

Outdoor pool, Pilligertorstraße, ✆ 2440

The Maifeld, as this fertile landscape is known, has been settled since the earliest times. Many of the place names are derived from Celtic origins. The Romans also used the area extensively. Caesar is said to have spent time in a castellum here before he set out for his second crossing of the Rhine. It has also been established that the Emperor Augustus had his stepson Drusus build an armory to help defend the borders to the Rhine. Caligula is believed to have been born in this armory.

This Roman military depot eventually became a Frankish royal court. After Christianity came to the area, the bishop Magnericus built a church in 580, to honor the Frankish religious figure, St. Martin. In the 7th century the bishop Modoald established a religious community, which soon evolved into an Augustine monastery. In 952 the relics of St. Severin were brought by ship from Trier to Hatzenport.

The many pilgrims visiting Münstermaifeld made a new church necessary. This church was completed in 1103, with St. Severus its second patron saint. The office of monastery provost was a popular one, because it included a wealthy benefice. Nikolaus von Cues also held the office and wrote many of his works here. Beginning in 1515 the monastery and its revenues belonged to the Archbishops of Trier, who let it be administered by their deans. The monastery members were secular and lived in stylish private houses, some of which survive to this day.

To leave Münstermaifeld and return to the Moselle at Hatzenport, cross the **Münsterplatz** uphill to the right and ride behind the church ⌁ continue past the small park ⌁ at the intersection turn right into the **Stiftsstraße** ⌁ at the next intersection turn left into the **Probsteihof** ⌁ keep right by the water tower and cross the Frankenstraße ⌁ ride into the side street, which makes a right bend before passing the last of the houses and taking you between fields out of Münstermaifeld ⌁ at the intersection continue straight, slightly offset to the right ⌁ turn right at the T-intersection ⌁ turn left at the next T-intersection ⌁ you now ride through the Schrumpf valley ⌁ follow the many curves of the Schrumpf stream, passing one mill after another, only a few of which have retained their original form ⌁ when you arrive in Hatzenport, ride under the railway and proceed down to the main road and rejoin the main cycle route on the bike lane in the road.

To continue along the main route from Moselkern, simply follow the

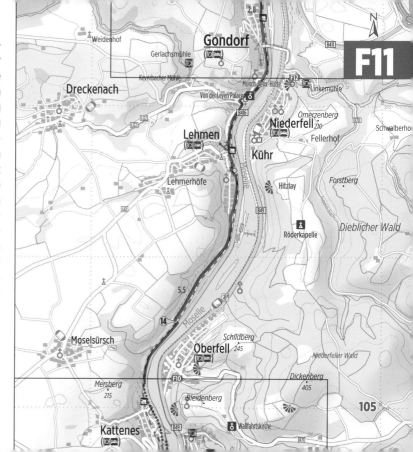

bicycle lane along the main road ～ you soon pass below Burg Bischofstein.

Burg Bischofstein

On a bluff above the river looms Bischofstein castle. Archbishop Arnold von Trier built the castle in the 12th century to protect his lands from the nobles from the Eifel and Hunsrück regions. Half way to the castle lies the 13th century chapel, "Pauluskapelle".

Continue along the bicycle lane to Hatzenport

Hatzenport

The old ferry tower recalls the days when a ferry crossed the river here, now replaced by the bridge in Löf, a little further downstream.

Hatzenport to Koblenz   27.5 km

Continue along the bicycle lane past Hatzenport and on to Löf.

Löf

You follow the bicycle lane along the river through Löf ～ **13** you ride under the road bridge ～ continue to Kattenes.

Kattenes

As you reach the first houses the bicycle lane changes to the left side of the road ～ continue on the bicycle path along the left side of the main road as you leave Kattenes ～ **14** the path takes you under the railway easement and then along the left side of the railway line into Lehmen.

Lehmen

Follow the street **Im Oberdorf** ～ this becomes the **Hauptstraße**, which you follow away from the railway tracks ～ keep right at the intersection to stay on the Hauptstraße through the centre of the village ～ keep left where the

road divides as you pass the last houses ～ the road makes a left bend and you reach Kobern-Gondorf ～ take the first turnoff to your right ～ simply follow this street through the town.

Kobern-Gondorf

Postal code: 56330; Area code: 02607

- 🄸 **Touristik und Kultur Kobern-Gondorf**, Lennigstr. 12-14, ✆ 1055, www.kobern-gondorf.de
- 🏛 **Wine Museum**, in the palace "von der Leyen", Gondorf. Open: Easter-Oct., Sat 11-14, Sun 14-16.
- 🕍 **Matthias chapel**, late Romanesque church (1230), in the Oberburg above Kobern.
- 🏰 **Von der Leyen Palace**, Ancestral water palace of the princes von Leyen, originally a water castle from the 11th c, the current buildings date mostly from the 14th and 16th c. Great damage has been done by leading the road and railway directly through the historic complex.
- 🏯 Castle ruins **Oberburg** and **Niederburg** (11th century).
- ✳ **Abteihof St. Marien**, Kobern, Kirchstr. 1, Germany's oldest surviving half-timbered structure (1320).
- ✳ **Romanesque defensive and clock tower** (1142), Kobern.

A narrow street winds through the crowded rows of houses that comprise Gondorf ～ you pass the Von der Leyen Palace ～ continue

Goloring

Wolken

F12

Güls 16

Karthause

Bisholder

Oberwe

Sauerbrunnen
Quidoborn
Euligerhof

Belltal

Bisholder Höhe
225

Rosenberg
285

Moselle

Dieblich

Lay

Layer Kopf
315

Matthias Chapel
Oberburg

Solligerhof

Niederburg

Winningen

Kühkopf
380

Museum Winningen

Abteihof St. Marien

Scheidterhof

Dieblichberg

Kandertal

Kobern

F11

Gondorf

Niederfell

Hinterberg

Gerlachsmühle

Bäckesberg

107

straight ahead under the road birdge into Kobern ~ take the bicycle path which begins on the right side of the street just after the railway station ~ to the right are the railway tracks ~ the bicycle path ends at the intersection ~ two streets continue straight ahead after this intersection, take the small street on the left ~ follow the street as it takes you through the **Marktplatz** and the historic old town, with its many half-timbered houses ~ follow the street as it becomes the **Marktstraße** ~ continue straight at the intersection ~ you pass a playing field as you ride out of the town ~ the street takes you between the railway line and the vineyards, which cling to the steep hillside that forms the outside of a long bend in the river. After the bend you pass under the tall freeway bridge that spans the entire Moselle valley ~ continue along the street towards Winningen ~ **15** ride straight into the **Uhlenweg**, past the small bridge over the railway line ~ continue along the **Marktstraße** to the **Marktplatz** in the centre of Winningen.

Winningen

Winningen

Postal code: 56333; Area code: 02606

🛈 **Touristik Winningen**, in the town hall, August-Horch-Straße 3, ☎ 2214, www.winningen.de

🏛 **Museum Winningen**, Schulstraße 5, ☎ 2126, Open: May-mid Nov., Sat, Sun 15-17 and by appointment. Local history and history of wine making, as well as the life and work of August Horch, the founder of Horch and Audi. Includes a collection of historic and modern engines.

✉ **Heated outdoor pool**, ☎ 670, on the Moselle.

Turn right at the end of the Marktplatz into the **Bachstraße** ~ turn left at the T-intersection in front of the railway tracks ~ ride straight across the intersection and follow the street beside the railway line out of Winningen ~ you

pass the church and the train station ~ and continue down the narrow lane between vineyards and railway until the valley flattens out and you reach Güls, a suburb of Koblenz ~ continue into the residential street ~ pass the church.

Güls

Turn right at the T-interection ~ immediately turn right ~ **16** after the Volksbank turn right into the **Stauseestraße** ~ follow this street back to the Moselle.

▎**CENTRE** To reach the centre of Koblenz it is best to use the pedestrian path on the railway bridge at Güls. To get onto the bridge, ride to the right by the river and right again after passing under the bridge. The precise route description into Koblenz can be found on page 132 and map G 13, as well as the city map on the following page.

To continue along the left bank, turn left by the river ~ there is a bicycle path along the right side of the street ~ continue along the bicycle lane as you enter Koblenz ~ **17** turn right onto the **Kurt-Schumacher-Brücke** and cross the

Moselle ～ follow the bicycle path off the bridge down to the street **Moselufer** ～ follow the bicycle path under the Kurt-Schumacher Bridge ～ a short distance after the bridge turn left, through the underpass and down to the river ～ follow the path to the right and ride along the river ～ pass the rowing club ～ continue along the river ～ you ride along the **Willy-Brandt-Ufer** 18 you reach a T-intersection with the **Pastor-Klein-Straße**, where you turn left ～ ride along the **Peter-Altmeier-Ufer** ～ you ride under the **Europabrücke**, the **railway bridge** and the **Balduinbrücke** ～ continue until you reach **Deutsches Eck**, where the Mosel flows into the Rhein.

The Rhine has its own special magic, born of the legend of the Nibelungen and many river freighters which come from much further south, bound for Europe's largest port, Rotterdam.

At this point the Moselle River Trail meets the Rhine Cycle Route.

Koblenz

Postal code: 56020; Area code: 0261

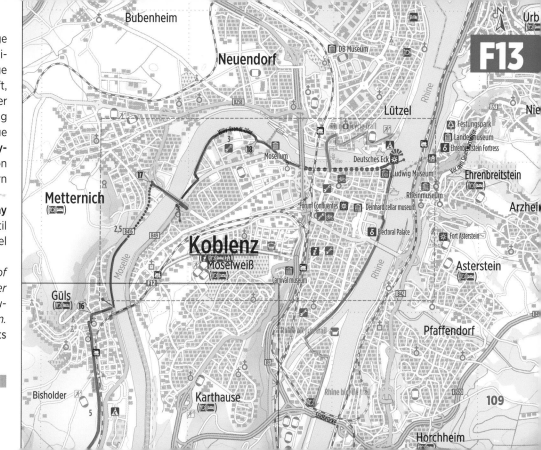

- 🛈 **Koblenz Touristik,** Bahnhofpl. 7, opposite the train station, ✆ 303880 or 31304, www.koblenz-touristik.de
- 🛈 **Tourist Information,** Forum Confluentes, Zentralplatz, ✆ 31304.
- ⚓ **Moselle and Rhine passenger ships,** Köln-Düsseldorfer Deutsche Rheinschifffahrt AG, ✆ 31030.
- ⚓ **Ferry Lützel-Deutsches Eck**. Operates: 15th Apr.-Sept.
- 🏛 **Landesmuseum,** in the Ehrenbreitstein fortress, ✆ 6675-0. Open: daily 9:30-17. Rotating exhibits and a comprehensive collection of technical artifacts.
- 🏛 **Mittelrhein-Museum,** Forum Confluentes, Zentralplatz, ✆ 1292520, Open: Tue-Sat 10:30-17, Sun/hol. 11-18. Displays with artifacts from the stone, bronze and iron ages, as well as Roman and Frankish times, plus artworks from the Gothic period to the Renaissance.
- 🏛 **Romanticum,** Forum Confluentes, Zentralplatz, ✆ 31304, Open: daily 10-18. Interactive exhibition covering the Rhine Romantic.
- 🏛 **Ludwig Museum,** Danziger Freiheit 1, ✆ 3040412, Open: Tue-Sat 10:30-17, Sun/hol. 11-18. Ludwig collection with emphasis on French modern art, also changing international exhibitions.
- 🏛 **Rheinmuseum,** Charlottenstr. 53a, ✆ 703450, Open: Tue-Sun 10-17. Exhibits about life on the Rhine.
- 🏛 **DB-Museum,** Schönbornsluster Str. 3, ✆ 396-1339, Open: Sat 10-16. German railway museum.
- 🏛 **Fastnachtsmuseum (Carnival Museum),** Fort Konstantin, Handwerkstr. 7a, Open: Sat, Sun 14-17.

Koblenz

- 🏛 **Deinhard Kellermuseum,** Deinhardplatz 3, ✆ 91151520, guided tours by arrangement.
- 🏛 **Mosellum,** Moselle barrage, Pastor-Klein-Str., ✆ 95234030, Open: Tue-Sun 10-17. Exhibitions covering the Moselle river, fishing, fish migration, shipping and hydroelectric power.
- 🛡 **Kurfürstliches Schloss (Prince elector's palace),** built 1777-86 for Prince Clemens Wenzeslaus von Trier, in the early-Classical style.
- 🛡 **Ehrenbreitstein fortress.** One of the largest fortifications in Europe with a large park, exhibition spaces and panorama view. A highlight is the cable car trip from the Deutsches Eck up to the fortress.
- ✳ **Koblenz cable car,** from the bank of the Rhine near the Deutsches Eck, the cable car takes you 890m across the river to the Ehren-breitstein fortress, 118 m above the river. Bicycles also transported.

- 📞 **Beatusbad,** Beatusstraße, ✆ 94249136
- 🚲 **Zangmeister,** Stegemannstr. 43, ✆ 98872450
- 🚲 **Fahrrad Franz,** Hohenfelder Str. 5, ✆ 91505-0
- 🚲 **Radsport Regenhardt,** Markenbildchenweg 28, ✆ 33667
- 🚲 **Sport Schmidt,** Poststr. 4, ✆ 28755200
- 🚲 **Rückenwind,** Gemüseg. 7, ✆ 70148061

The name Koblenz is derived from "confluentes," the Latin word for confluence. In the first century AD, Legionnaires of the Emperor Tiberius erected a fortress to protect the Moselle river crossing. The best view of the city and the confluence of the two rivers at the Deutsches Eck can be had from Ehrenbreitstein, the massive fortress high above the right bank of the Rhine. The fortress was designed by Prussian military engineers in the 19th century. Although the fortress and the palace face the Rhine, Koblenz was originally oriented primarily to the Moselle. This is evident in the old city, which expands away from the Florins market, the Plan, and the Münzplatz.

Koblenz

Lützel

Train station Lützel

Deutsches Eck

Ludwig Museum

Train station Ehrenbreitstein

Ehrenbreitstein

Rhine

Mosellum

Rauental

Goldgrube

Metternich

Moselle

St. Laurentus

Moselweiß

Train station Moselweiß

Forum Confluentes

Deinhard cellar museum

Electoral Palace

Town hall

Carneval Museum

Main station

St. Beatus

Cemetary of Allied Forces

111

400 m

Trierer Str.
Auf Im Bandt
Johnweg
Bachweg
Bachweg
In der Wied
Wedinanstr.
Isenburgstr.
Oberweiher
Trifterrothstr.
Oberweiher
Plenierweg
Kreweg
Geisbachstr.
Geisbachstraße

Willy-Brandt-Ufer
Pastor- Klein-Str.
Peter-Klöckner-Str.
Ludwig- Erhard-Str.
Schlachthofstraße
Friedrich- Syrup-Straße
Im Rauental
Hermannstr.
Jüdischer Friedhof
Burgstr.
Auf der Donne
Am Alten Hospital
Kastorhof
Rheinstr.
Konrad-
Stresemannstr.
Neustadt

Europabrücke
Baldunbrücke
Peter-Altmeier-Ufer

Rudolf-Virchow-Str.
Ferdinand-Sauerbruch-Str.
Koblenzer Str.
Behringstr.
Moselweißer Str.
St.-Elisabeth-Str.
St-Yorckstr.
Hoevelstr.

Kurt-Schumacher-Brücke
Moselufer
Moselring
Weißer
Altenhof
Markstr.
Firmungstr.
Entenpfuhl
Pfuhl
Löhrstr.
Clemensstr.
Viktoriastr.

Am Wollershof
Am Fort

Ring
Friedrich-Ebert-Ring
Schloßstr.
Schloßstr.
Stegemannstr.
Casinostr.
Voh Werth Str.
Rizzastr.
Bahnhofstr.
Roonstr.
Roonstr.
Mainzer Str.
Südallee
Hohenfelder
Kastorplatz

Layerstr.
Layerstr.
Koblenzer Str.-Heiligen weg
Bogenstr.
In der Goberüberg
Gutenberg
Overbergstr.
Cusanusstr.
Lindenstr.
Postamt
Am Fort

Sandgasse
Römerstraße
Hubertingsweg
Maigesetzweg
Cemetary of Allied Forces
Simmerner Straße
Hohenzollernstr.
Kurfürstenstr.
Mainzer Str.
Bismarckstr.

Bernkastel-Kues to Koblenz on the right bank 127 km

The last section anlong the right bank also has plenty to offer, such as the Stubern Monastery ruins or Thurant Castle. Once again, one should not miss tasting the wonderful wines of the Moselle valley, even if the amusing and creative names such as "Graacher Himmelreich", "Zeller Schwarze Katz" oder "Bullayer Brautrock" mean little to those not versed in German. You will ride some of the most famous and beautiful towns along the Moselle, such as Zell an der Mosel, Zeltingen-Rachtig and especially Beilstein, which has written film history thanks to its enchanting appearance. As you reach the end of the Moselle River trail you can take in the city centre of Koblenz and the confluence of the Moselle and the Rhein.

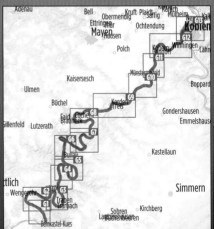

The route in this section takes you along flat and paved bicycle paths, bicycle lanes and quiet streets. The route is only unpaved between the towns of Bullay and Senheim as well as Cond and Treis-Karden, as the route takes you through a nature reserve.

The main route follows the right bank as far as Zell, where it changes to the left bank. Between Treis-Karden and Alken it once more follows the right bank, switching to the left bank for the rest of the distance to Koblenz.

Bernkastel-Kues, St. Nikolaus Hospital

Bernkastel-Kues   see page 70

Bernkastel-Kues
to Traben-Trarbach   **22 km**

1 Ride under the bridge and continue to the end of the parking area ∿ keep left at the fork and continue beside the river ∿ as you reach Graach continue straight ahead along the river.

CENTRE The quaint village of Graach is certainly worth a visit. To reach the centre turn right after the caravan parking area and ride through the underpass.

Graach

Postal code: 54470; Area code: 06531

🛈 **Touristikbüro**, Hauptstr. 94 ✆ 2541, www.graach.de

🏛 **Wine Museum Walter Frank**, ✆ 3273, Open: daily by arrangement. Exhibits of historic tools used in growing and making wine.

🏛 **Local History Museum**, in the Mattheiser Hof, corner Kirchstraße/Gestade, ✆ 8462, Open: Jul.-Oct., Wed and Sat 15-17. A trip into the history of Graach.

Ancient wine estates line the road, and in the narrow alleys the vines seem to be everywhere. Graach is a charming village for falling in love and lingering on the sunny side of the river. It is no wonder

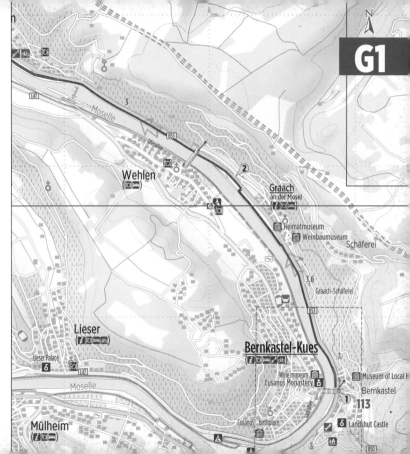

G1

113

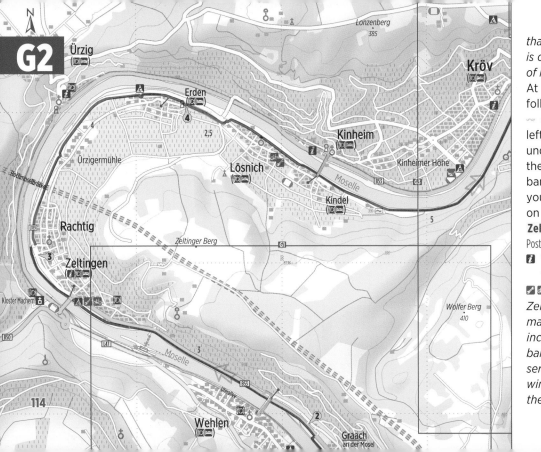

that the best-known vineyard in the village is called Graacher Himmelreich, or kingdom of heaven.

At the other end of Graach, turn right and follow the path back up to the main road **2** ~ continue on the bicycle path along the left side of the main road ~ after passing under the bridge the bicycle path leaves the main road and takes you along the river bank all the way to Zeltingen-Rachtig ~ as you reach the village you ride past a barrage on the river.

Zeltingen-Rachtig

Postal code: 54492; Area code: 06532

i **Verkehrsbüro**, Uferallee 13, *☎* 2404, www.zeltingen-rachtig.de

Fahrräder Wildmann, Uferallee 55, *☎* 954367

Zeltingen is another charming village with many impressive residences and estates, including fine examples of the Moselle's baroque architecture. This village has preserved the characteristic flavor of an old wine-making community better than some of the other towns and villages along the river.

And the atmosphere is especially festive during the traditional annual wine festival.

German knights settled in Rachtig in 1247, and built the handsome manor house, a significant late-gothic secular building. The distinctive church of red sandstone recalls a Romanesque house of worship, but it was actually built only in 1906. The tower, however, is older, dating to the 18th century.

Continue along the bicycle and pedestrian path through the park on the river ∿ straight ahead under the bridge ∿ **3** as you reach the underpass, turn right and ride under the main road ∿ immediately turn left ∿ follow the street ∿ ride straight at the intersection ∿ follow the paved lane along the right side of the main road out of Rachtig ∿ you soon reach Ürzigermühle.

Ürzigermühle

Ride straight at the intersection ∿ continue along the lane between fields and the main road into Erden ∿ ride straight at the intersection, then immediately left to continue on the lane beside the main road.

Erden

You ride past Erden, between the main road and the houses ∿ **4** turn left in the direction of Lösnich and traben-Trarbach at the T-intersection ∿ you leave Erden ∿ ride straight ahead through the **roundabout** into Lösnich ∿ turn left into the first side street, **Gestade** ∿ you follow the street between the houses and a park.

Lösnich

Postal code: 54492; Area code: 06532

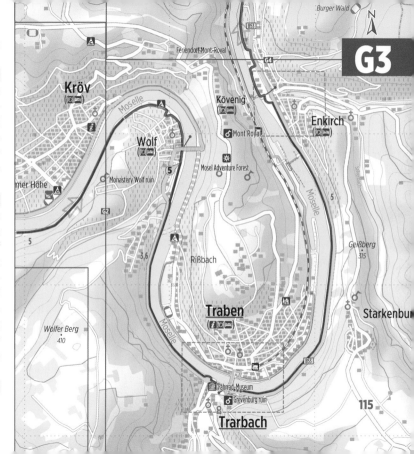

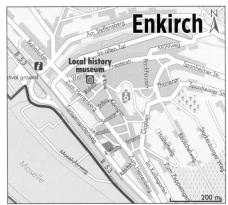

Enkirch

N

🚲 ♿ **Fahrrad Warscheid**, Hauptstr. 73, 📞 1790

Lösnich borders seamlessly with the next village, Kindel.

Kindel

Postal code: 54538; Area code: 06532

ℹ️ **Tourist Information Kinheim**, Moselweinstr. 14, 📞 3444, www.kinheim.de

Keep left where the street curves to the right ∿ ride under the bridge and follow the paved lane out of Kindel ∿ continue on the bicycle path along the river towards Wolf

∿ you pass a camping ground just before entering the village.

Wolf

Turn left at the T-intersection onto the street **Im Luxgraben** ∿ follow the street next to the river past the houses of Wolf ∿ ride under the bridge ∿ **5** continue straight where the road bends to the right ∿ turn left at the T-intersection ∿ the bicycle path now takes you along the left side of the main road towards Traben-Trarbach.

⚠️ A new bridge across the Moselle is under construction here until at least 2015, so there may be a small detour required to avoid building works.

Traben-Trarbach   see page 88

Traben-Trarbach to Zell   19.5 km

Keep left by the roundabout in Trarbach ∿ ride straight through the parking area and under the road bridge ∿ continue out of Trarbach on the bicycle path along the B 53 ∿ as you reach Enkirch you pass a barrage ∿ continue straight ahead beside the main road.

Enkirch

Postal code: 56850; Area code: 06541

ℹ️ **Verkehrsbüro**, 📞 9265, www.enkirch.de

⛴️ **Ferry across the Moselle**, Operates: Easter-Oct., daily 9-12 & 13-18:30

🏛️ **Heimatstuben Museum (Local history museum)**, in the Ratsweinschenke, Weing. 20, 📞 9265, Open: Fri, Sat 17-19, Sun 11-12. Exhibits of historic trades and workshops as well as a collection of minerals.

The solidly-made stone buildings and half-timbered houses testify to the generosity of the Sponheimers, who lived in the nearby Starkenburg. Enkirch is also distinguished by the highly developed trades that prospered in the town.

Impressive old houses, traces of the town's old defensive fortification, the "Drilles," a revolving cage for punishing people, and the period chambers in the Ratsweinschenke give glimpses into village life in the 15th to 17th centuries.

▌In Enkirch you have the opportunity of taking a ferry to the other bank.

Turn left after rounding an upramp by the main road ⁓ you pass the ferry landing ⁓ follow the paved path along the river and then back beside the main road ⁓ turn left shortly after passing an underpass ⁓ follow the lane, which takes you between the river and the vinyards almost all the way to the village of Burg **6** turn right at the fork.

CENTRE To ride through the centre of Burg, keep left at the fork. Turn right and ride through the underpass after the playing field, then turn left at the T-intersection and ride along the main street to the other end of the village, where you rejoin the main route along the main road.

Ride up to the main road and turn left onto the bicycle path ⁓ you follow the path along the main road past Burg.

Burg

Postal code: 56843; Area code: 06541

ℹ Tourist-Information, Schulstr. 8, ✆ 811420, www.burg-mosel.de

Ⓐ Wine educational trail.

Continue on the bicycle path beside the main road ⁓ you pass under a road bridge ⁓ turn left a short distance after the bridge ⁓ you now continue along a field road parallel to the main road ⁓ follow the left and right bends in the lane as you ride between vinyards ⁓ turn left before the playing field towards Zell and Pünderich **7** turn to the right in front of the camping ground "Moselland" ⁓ follow the lane between vinyards and the river ⁓ you pass a park and playground as you reach Pünderich.

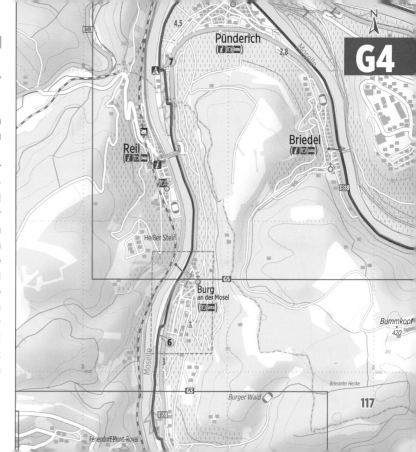

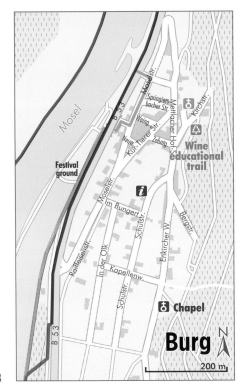

Festival ground

Wine educational trail

Chapel

Burg N

200 m

Pünderich

Postal code: 56862; Area code: 06542

🛈 **Tourist Information,** ✆ 900021, www.puenderich.de

⚓ **Ferry across the Moselle,** for timetable information ✆ 900020 or 900021.

One of the best-known photo motifs along the Moselle is the old ferry house in Pünderich. Built in 1621, it and the neighboring half-timbered buildings are particularly picturesque. An inscription on the Rathaus bears the words, "Fred in disem Huis, Ders nit helt bleib drus!" which amounts to a warning not to enter unless you can hold your wine. Nevertheless, we suggest this idyllic village is an excellent place to sample some of the local wines.

TIP You once again have the opportunity to take a ferry to the other river bank. Local people still call it the "Ponte," from the Latin word for ferry.

Continue between the park and houses past the ferry landing ⌇ by the camping ground "Ma-

rienburg" follow the left and right bends, which takes you onto a path directly along the bank of the river ⌇ after leaving Pünderich behind it is a short ride before reaching Briedel, which stretches along the other side of the main road. The historic town centre lies directly opposite the ferry landing.

Briedel

Postal code: 56867; Area code: 06542

🛈 **Tourist Information,** Bergstr. 2, ✆ 4013, www.briedel.de

⚓ **Ferry across the Moselle,** for timetable information ✆ 4640 or 4613

Zell a. d. Mosel

View into the Moselle valley towards Briedel

Continue on the path along the shoreline, which after Briedel is often in the shade of the forest that covers the slopes rising from the river ∼ ride under the road bridge leading to Kaimt ∼ continue on the bicycle path along the river ∼ the path takes you up to a street where you ride to the left through Zell.

Zell

Postal code: 56856; Area code: 06542

- 🛈 **Zeller Land Tourismus GmbH**, Balduinstr. 44, town hall, ☎ 96220, www.zellerland.de or www.zell-mosel.com
- ⛴ **Moselle passenger ships, Gebr. Kolb,** ☎ 5335, Zell-Cochem-Bernkastel-Kues and return.

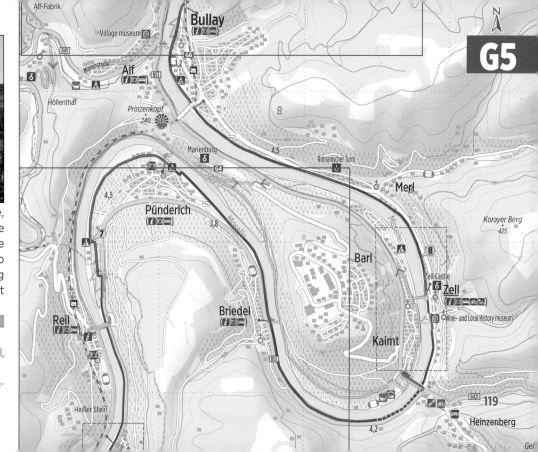

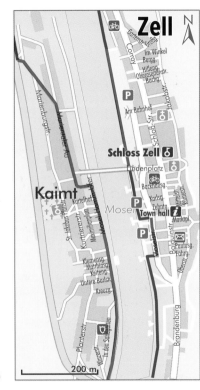

Zell

Kaimt

200 m

🏛 **Wein- und Heimatmuseum** (Wine and local history museum), town hall, ☎ 96960, Open: Wed, Sat 14:30-17.

🏰 **Schloss Zell**, palace erected 1535-1543, today a hotel.

🚲 **Zweirad Klaus**, Notenau 11, ☎ 9899-0, also E-bikes

Like Traben-Trarbach, Zell was often the scene of disastrous fires. As a result relatively few structures from the middle ages survived. Among the buildings that distinguish Zell are the 15th century palace which today is a hotel, and the Caspary house in the Balduinstraße. Particularly striking are two towers, one round and the other rectangular, that rise from the vineyards. These are remains for the town's old defensive walls.

Across the pedestrian bridge lies Kaimt, and the residence of the Boos von Waldeck. The distinctive half-timbered house with the tall gable was the summer home of the family that held Burg Waldeck in the Hunsrück. Count Ludwig Josef von Boos zu Waldeck and Montfort was the last Oberamtmann, a senior public official, in Zell. The house was purchased by the court administrator in 1824, and passed by marriage in 1889 to

View towards Merl

the Treis family, which operates the vineyard to this day.

This vineyard is not the only interesting sight here. With about 4.5 million grape vines, Zell is one of the largest wine producing communities on the Moselle.

One of the best known wines is the "Zeller Schwarze Katz," (black cat) produced with grapes from 16 different locations. A sculpture on the fountain of the market square shows a snarling cat on top of a wine barrel.

The Zeller Schwarze Katz

The best-known and most-told story about the "black cat" is based on something that is said to have occurred in the cellars of the Mayntzer vinyard in the 19th century. Wine merchants were highly respected people, who understood a great deal about wine and personally visited the vinyards and cellars as they searched for the best vintages.

The story is that three wine merchants from Aachen were in the wine cellars of the Mayntzer vinyards. They were about to conclude their negotiations, but even after repeatedly sampling the wines, they could not agree which of three cartloads of wine was the best. The excited atmosphere in the cellar was just one indication of

Bullay

how diligently the merchants had been sampling the wines, when the vintner's wife, accompanied by a black cat, came into the cellar with a meal intended to help the merchants reach an decision. As the owner of the vineyards attempted to siphon some more wine from one of the barrels, the cat leapt onto the barrel and stood there snarling, with its back arched and claws outstretched. It refused to allow anyone near the wine. Finally the merchants, who had long ago realized this was the best wine, had to admit the cat was right and they purchased the wine without trying it again. They called the wine "Zeller Schwarze Katz," and it turned out to be very popular. When that news reached the vintners of Zell, they adopted the name for their best wines.

"Bullayer Brautrock"

Zell to Beilstein   26.5 km

TIP The official main route changes to the left bank in Zell. The route description can be found on page 92.

Keep left after the narrow pedestrian bridge and continue along the river through the car parking areas ➔ 8 the lane becomes a bicycle and pedestrian path, which takes you directly along the shoreline to Merl.

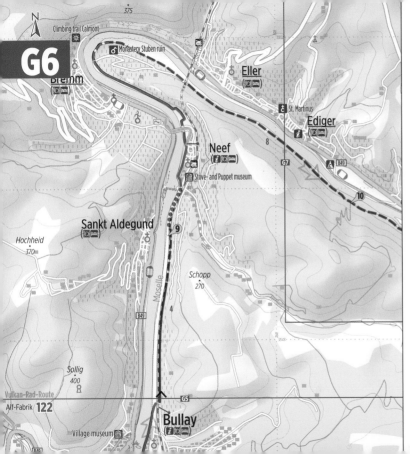

G6

Climbing trail Calmont
Monastery Stuben ruin
Bremm
Eller
St. Martinus
Ediger
Neef
Stove- and Puppet museum
Sankt Aldegund
Hochheid 370
Schopp 270
Moselle
B49
Sollig 400

Bullay
Village museum

Merl

One landmark visible from afar is the 12th century Romanesque tower.

Continue on the bicycle path along the river past Merl ~ you ride past vinyards on your way to Bullay ~ keep left and ride under the double decker road and rail bridge ~ you pass a camping ground and a playing field as you continue along the river ~ the centre of the town lies to your right.

Bullay

Postal code: 56859; Area code: 06542

ℹ **Tourist Information,** ✆ 21141, www.bullay.de

⚓ **Passenger ferry Alf-Bullay,** ✆ 22352 or 0175/8869724, Operates: Mar.-Apr., Thur-Tue 7:30-17, May-15th Nov., daily 7:30-19.

Stuben Monastery Ruins by Bremm

Bullay, formerly the Roman settlement of Boletum, was a free city by the beginning of the 12th century, and as such the property of the Lords of Arras, who occupied the castle across the Moselle and up the valley of the Alf stream. The privileges associated with this status elevated Bullay above the valley's other towns and villages, which all belonged to the prince in Trier and his abbots.

The name of the wine from this area, the "Bullayer Brautrock" (bride's gown) is derived from a story that relates to the local count's sense of independence. Toward the end of the 16th century, the count's treasury was once again virtually empty because the community had celebrated too many expensive festivals.

The count's son wished to marry the daughter of a local knight, but could not afford it. So the bride's father agreed to give his future son-in-law a vineyard with which he could pay for the bride's wedding gown. But he attached a condition, which was that the proceeds from the vineyard should always belong to his daughter. This enabled her to assure her future security in case the young count should prove wasteful with his money. Continue along the river bank until you reach the main road ～ cross the road and ride through the railway underpass ～ immediately turn left into the lane between the railway line and the vinyards ～ follow the lane parallel to the railway line ～ **9** you ride back under the railway ～ turn right onto the main road **K 41** and ride into Neef.

View towards Briedern

Neef

Postal code: 56858; Area code: 06542

🛈 **Tourist Information,** ✆ 21575, www.weinortneef.de

🏛 **Oven und Doll Museum,** Neugartenstr. 6. Collection of about 350 antique dolls, 126 teddy bears, dolls houses and other toys as well as historic household appliances and 60 cast iron stoves from 3 centuries.

Follow the street along the river ∼ you pass a barrage ∼ at the other end of the town turn left off the main road before it leads up to the bridge.

ATTENTION The route along the unpaved path after the Stuben Monastery ruins can be difficult to pass after heavy rainfall, in which case you would be advised to cross the bridge at Neef to the route along the left bank.

To continue on the right bank ride under the bridge ∼ follow the paved lane as it takes you between the river and the vinyards ∼ at the end of the steep embankment continue straight into the unpaved track ∼ you follow the inside of the river bend and pass the Ruins of the Stuben Monastery.

Stuben Monastery Ruins

Amid the grape vines stands the ruins of a monastery that was founded in 1136. A relic from the holy cross, which the knight Heinrich von Ulmen had stolen from Byzantium in 1204, was kept here until 1794. Today the relic can be seen in the cathedral at Limburg.

Continue along the unpaved track ∼ ride under the railway bridge ∼ the track takes you through forest along the edge

Beilstein

of the river ∼ **10** keep left at the fork in the track ∼ you emerge at a T-intersection in front of vinyards ∼ turn left and ride along the paved lane ∼ at the fork turn left into the unpaved track ∼ this takes you past orchards to a bridge and the first houses of Senheim ∼ turn right in front of the bridge and follow this street into the centre of senheim.

Senheim

Postal code: 56820; Area code: 02673

🛈 **Local council,** ✆ 962197 or **Heimat und Verkehrsverein,** Senheim-Senhals, ✆ 962820, www.senheim.de

🏛 **Weinmuseum,** Schlagkamp-Desoye Winery, Zeller Str. 186, ✆ 4381, Open: daily 8-12 & 14-18:30. Tours of the vineyard, history and wine tasting.

Turn left at the main street, **Brunnenstraße**, in the centre of Senheim and ride out to the main road ∼ turn right ∼ follow the bicycle lane which runs along the left side of the main road towards Mesenich

Beilstein

~ just before Mesenich you come to follow a bicycle path between the main road and the river ~ this takes you along the river past the town.

Mesenich
The path takes you away from the road as you leave Mesenich ~ **11** you ride past a camping ground ~ simply follow the path between the vinyards and the river all the way to Briedern.

Briedern
Although you can barely see over the grape vines, it becomes evident that not every square metre of the hillsides are being used

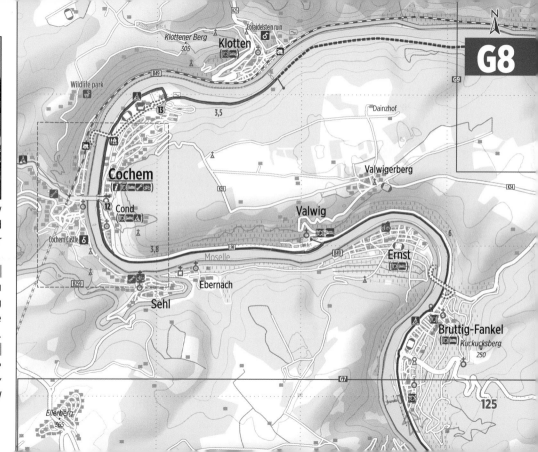

Klottener Berg
305

Klotten

Coraidelstein ruin

Wildlife park

Dainzhof

13

3,5

Cochem

Valwigerberg

12 Cond

Valwig

Cochem Castle 6

3,8

Moselle

Ernst

Ebernach

Sehl

Bruttig-Fankel

Kuckucksberg
250

Ellerberg
365

to grow grapes. Some areas have even been cleared of their vines, lie fallow or have been replanted with trees.

Ride straight onto the street along the waterfront ～ follow this street to the main road at the other end of the village ～ ride straight ahead onto the bicycle path along the left side of the main road ～ follow the path to Beilstein.

Beilstein

Postal code: 56814; Area code: 02673

- ℹ **Verkehrsverein,** Bachstr. 47, ☎ 900191, www.beilstein-mosel.de
- ⛴ **Ferry Beilstein-Ellenz-Poltersdorf,** ☎ 1515, Operates: daily 9-12 & 13-18.
- 🏰 **Metternich Castle,** can only be reached on foot, Open: Apr.-Oct., Mon-Sun 8:30-18:30.

The name of the village Beilstein goes way back in history. One of the oldest forms of hunting, dating to prehistoric times, includes a method the locals call "beieln." Hunters use noise and fire to drive animals into a funnel formed by helpers. This funnel leads to a cliff, which the panicked animals plunge down to

View over Treis-Karden

their deaths. It was at just such a "beyhel-stein" that the village was established in the 14th century.

The appealing little village even went into German filmmaking history as the setting for "Rothenburg an der Mosel." Five movies have been filmed here.

Towering over the tiny community is the imposing ruin of Metternich castle. The first owner of the castle was the knight Cuno von Beyhelstein, as a document from the year 1129 proves. In 1268 the Braunshorns from the Hunsrück were granted title to the castle. One

Johann von Braunshorn won the status of city for Beilstein, built fortifications and brought ten Jewish families to the community. Wine, slate and agricultural products were traded at the market, helping the city establish great wealth.

The Braunshorns died out, however, and the Winneburgers from Cochem took control of the estate. After the Thirty Years War and the religious upheavals of the period, control of the town passed to Trier, which granted the property to the Baron von Metternich. Klemens Wenzel Metternich, the Austrian statesman who dominated European politics in the early 19th century, was the last owner of this castle.

Beilstein to Treis-Karden   21 km

You pass the village of Beilstein ～ continue on the bicycle path beside the main road to Bruttig-Fankel.

Bruttig-Fankel

Follow bicycle path along the main road past the town ～ here you pass a barrage and

Eltz Castle

Pilliger Heck

Ringelsteiner Mühle

Müdenerberg

Dömpel
270

Moselkern

B416 3,6

Klickerterhof

Brieden

Kail

Müden

Eichenberg
270

Moselle

St. Castor

Monastery museum

Karden

Pommerer Mart
270

Archäologiepark Martberg

Fahrlei
265

Zilleskapelle

4,2

Pommern

1,6

B49

Treis

14

L108

Kesselkopf
280

Schock
425

Traiser Berg
470

Lütz

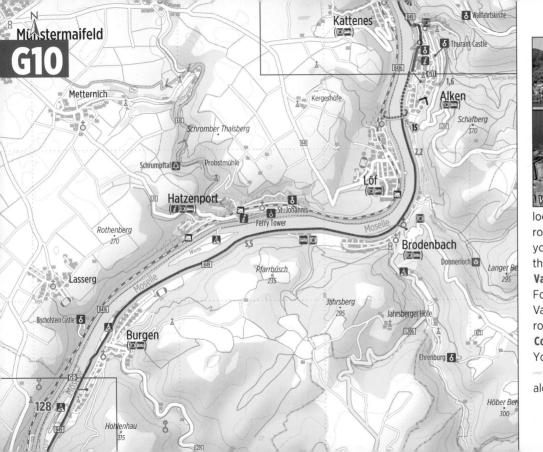

Kattenes

B49

Wallfahrtskirche

Thurant Castle

Metternich

Kergeshöfe

Alken

Schromber Thalsberg

Schafberg
370

Schrumpftal

Probstmühle

Löf

Hatzenport

St. Johannis

Ferry Tower

Moselle

Brodenbach

Rothenberg
270

Werth

Donnerloch

Langer Be
295

Lasserg

Moselle

B49

Pfarrbüsch
235

Jahrsberg
295

Jahrsberger Höfe

Bischofstein Castle

B416

Burgen

Ehrenburg

Höber Ber
300

Hohlenhau
315

View towards Karden

locks on the river ⁓ continue straight at the roundabout ⁓ as you pass the last houses you ride under a road bridge ⁓ continue on the bicycle path to Valwig.

Valwig

Follow the bicycle and pedestrian path past Valwig ⁓ the path takes you between the road and the river to Cochem-Cond.

Cochem-Cond   see page 98

You ride along the waterside in Cochem-Cond ⁓ you pass under a road bridge **12** ⁓ continue along the bicycle path to the next road bridge.

Between Cochem-Cond and Treis-Karden the route along the right bank follows an unpaved path through a nature reserve. This path can become difficult to pass after heavy rainfall, in which case you would be advised to cross the bridge here to the route along the left bank. To continue on the right bank ride under the bridge ～ you pass a playing field and outdoor pool ～ by the camping ground the path ends and you continue on a small street ～ after a right bend you reach a roundabout ～ **13** turn left and ride along a paved lane through the forest and along the Moselle ～ you reach a ferry opposite Klotten.

You can take the ferry to Klotten on the opposite bank of the Moselle.

After the ferry follow the unpaved path ～ this takes you along the river through a nature reserve, where you can now enjoy a long, quiet ride through a tranquill riverside landscape ～ after passing a gate the route is once more paved ～ ride past the light industrial area and shops ～ keep right at the intersection, where going left leads to the marina and camping ground ～ after the small bridge you reach the houses of Treis-Karden ～ **14** turn left in the direction of Cochem, Koblenz and Kaisersesch ～ ride along the main street through the town.

Treis-Karden see page 100

Treis-Karden to Niederfell **21.5 km**

You pass the market square ～ continue straight ahead to the roundabout by the bridge ～ take the first exit and follow the bicycle path along the left side of the **B 49** towards Burgen ～ after

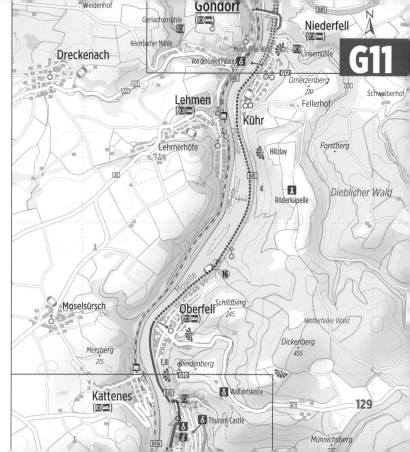

G11

129

about a thrid of the way you pass a few houses by the Müden barrage and locks ~ you pass a camping ground as you eventually reach Burgen.

Burgen

Follow the bicycle path along the main road past Burgen ~ you pass a camping ground once again as you leave the village ~ continue along the bicycle path to Brodenbach.

Brodenbach

Follow the bicycle path past Brodenbach ~ continue towards Alken ~ **15** you pass under a road bridge.

> **TIP** The official main route changes to the left bank across this bridge. The route description can be found on page 106.

Continue along the bicycle path to the first houses of Alken ~ here you must cross the road to continue on the bicycle path along the right side of the road.

Alken

Postal code: 56332; Area code: 02605

🄸 **Tourist Information Untermosel,** ✆ 02607/4927, www.sonnige-untermosel.de, www.alken.de

🄱 **St. Michael,** ✆ 1298 or 8997, Open: Easter-Oct, Sun/hol. 14-17.

🄲 **Thurant Castle,** ✆ 2004, Open: Mar.-Apr., 10-17, May-Oct., 10-18, Nov.-Feb., 10-16. Begun in 1197, it was besieged in 1246-1248. The peace contract from 1248 is today one of the oldest surviving documents in the German language.

🏧 **R. Ammann,** Mittelstr. 9, 960241

EXCURSION From Alken you can make an excursion to Thurant Castle above the town. Turn right onto the L 207 before entering Alken, after the second turn a small road to the left leads to the castle.

Thurant Castle

Entering Burg Thurant presents the visitor with a mixture of the old and the new. The Allmers family acquired the ruins in 1911 and rebuilt the property. You first take a bridge into the forecourt of the castle. Next comes the main courtyard, with a chapel that holds the Allmers' tomb. The Trier Tower dominates the courtyard, a reminder of the days when the Archbishops of Trier and Cologne shared the castle. A massive wall separated the properties of the two bishops, and made two gates necessary. That is why the castle today has a Cologne Tower and a Trier Tower.

If one keeps going, you reach the so-called Rose Garden in the older part of the castle. Here are the ruins of a banquet hall and two round towers that are connected by a parapet. The 23 coats of arms of the local gentry can be seen in one of the towers. Off the parapet there is a hunting lodge with trophies and weapons. Finally you reach the Cologne Tower, with its frightful torture chamber and dungeon.

Continue along the pedestrian zone through Alken ~ at the far end of the town you must cross the road once more ~ continue on the bicycle path on the left side of the road towards Oberfell.

Oberfell

Follow the bicycle lane along the main road through Oberfell ~ **16** you pass a playing field as you leave the town ~ continue along the bicycle lane to Niederfell.

Wolken

Bisholder

Karthause

Bisholder Höhe
225

Oberwerth

G13

3,5

Sauerbrunnen

Quidoborn

Euligerhof

Rosenberg
285

Belltal

Moselle

17

Lay

B416

B327

Layer Kopf
315

B9

Dieblich

Winningen

Matthias Chapel

Oberburg

Niederburg

Abteihof St. Marien

Museum Winningen

Kobern

Dieblichberg

6,5

2,8

Kandertal

Kühkopf
380

Stolzenfels Castle

Gondorf

G11

B411

Niederfell

Hinterberg
235

Stolzenfe

Stolzenfels-Kapelle

Bäckesberg

Mönch-Felix-Hütte

Linkemühle

Von der Leyen Palace

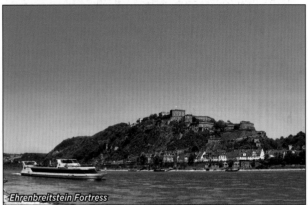
Ehrenbreitstein Fortress

Niederfell

Niederfell to Koblenz   16.5 km

ATTENTION ⚠ Please be aware that the route ahead follows a very narrow bicycle lane between Dieblich and Lay, then continues with heavy traffic to Koblenz. We recommend crossing the river over the next bridge and continuing your journey to Koblenz on the route along the left bank in order to avoid this dangerous section.

If you are continung along the right bank, ride on the bicycle lane along the main road past Niederfell ～ after passing the last houses you ride under the bridge which leads over the Moselle to Kobern-Gondorf ～ continue to Dieblich.

Dieblich

Continue along the B 49 past Dieblich ～ here the bicycle lane becomes quite narrow ～ after the town you ride under the extremely tall freeway bridge which spans the entire Moselle valley here ～ continue along the bicycle lane beside the main road to Lay.

Lay

🚢 **Ferry**, currently out of operation.

Ride into Lay along the bicycle lane, which takes you as far as the ferry landing.

ATTENTION If the ferry is operating, we recommend crossing the river and continuing your journey to Koblenz on the route along the left bank in order to avoid the route along busy road on the right bank.

To continue on the right bank, follow the main road out of Lay ～ **17** the bicycle lane ends and only a narrow strip, not intended as a bicycle lane, helps keep you out of the traffic ～ continue to the railway and pedestrian bridge in Koblenz.

ALTERNATIVE If you continue straight here you come to the Kurt-Schumacher-Brücke. From there you can continue to the "Deutsches Eck," where the Moselle flows into the Rhein. The route description can be found on page 109. To ride into the centre, turn right in front of the railway and pedestrian bridge ～ ride up to an intersection ～ continue straight into the **Unterbreitweg** ～ this becomes a residential street ～ continue to the T-intersection ～ **18** turn left here and then right into the next side street, **Beatusstraße** ～ ride on the bicycle path along this street all the way to a large intersection below an elevated roadway ～ turn left onto the **Simmerner Straße** ～ follow the path to the next large

Deutsche Eck in Koblenz

intersection ⁓ **19** turn right here ⁓ ride below the three bridges ⁓ immediately turn right into **Löhrstraße** ⁓ follow this street to the **20** Koblenz train station.

Koblenz see page 109

You have now reached the end of this cycling journey. We hope that you had an enjoyable and experience-rich cycling tour and are happy that you have chosen a bikeline-Cycling Guide to accompany you on your journey.

The *bikeline*-Team wishes you a safe and enjoyable return trip!

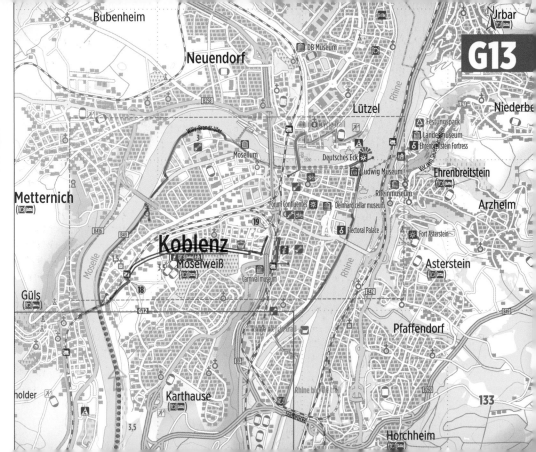

Overnight accommodation

The following list includes accommodation in the following categories:

H	Hotel
Hg	Hotel garni
Gh	Inn
P	Pension
Pz	Private room
BB	Bed and Breakfast
Fw	Vacation home (selected)
Bh	Farm
Hh	Hay hotel
🏠	Youth Hostel
🅰	Campground
▲	Tent site

We have not attempted to list every possible place where visitors can spend the night, and listings should not be construed as any kind of recommendation. The Roman number (I-VII) after the telephone number indicates price range. These fall into six categories, listed below, and do not necessarily reflect the relative comfort and quality available:

I	less than € 15
II	€ 15 to € 23
III	€ 23 to € 30
IV	€ 30 to € 35
V	€ 35 to € 50
VI	€ 50 to € 70
VII	over € 70

These categories are based on the price per person in a double room equipped with shower or bath, with breakfast, unless otherwise indicated. Rooms with bath or shower in the hall are indicated with the symbol 🛁. The symbol 🔄 indicates ADFC-certified, cyclist-friendly BettBike accommodation. Because we wish to expand this list and keep it up-to-date, we welcome any comments, additions or corrections you may have. There is no charge for a listing.

Metz (F)
Postal code: 57007; Area code: 0387
🛈 Office de tourisme cathedrale, 2, Place d'Armes, ✆ 555376
🛈 Moselle Tourisme, 2-4, rue de Pont Moreau, ✆ 375780
H Alérion Hôtel Centre Gare, 20, rue Gambetta, ✆ 667403, IV-V
H All Seasons, 23, avenue Foch, ✆ 668111, V-VII
H Balladins, 20, rue Gambetta, ✆ 667403, II-III
H Best Hotel, 3, rue Pierre Boileau, ✆ 331956, III
H Bristol, 7, rue Lafayette, ✆ 667422, III
H Campanile Technopole, 2, boulevard Solidarité, ✆ 751311, IV-V
H Cécil, 14, rue Pasteur, ✆ 666613, IV
H Centre Routier Arcotel, 55, avenue des deux Fontaines, ✆ 325326, I-II
H de la Cathédrale, 25, place de Chambre, ✆ 750002, V
H du Centre, 14, rue Dupont des Loges, ✆ 360693, III
H du Nord, 173a, route de Thionville, ✆ 325329, II-III
H du Théâtre, 3, rue du Pont Saint-Marcel, ✆ 311010, V-VII
H Escurial, 18, rue Pasteur, ✆ 664096, IV-V
H Foch, 8, avenue Foch, ✆ 744075, III
H Formule 1, 13, rue des Selliers, ✆ 089/1705314, III
H Grand Hotel de Metz, 3, rue des Clercs, ✆ 361633, V-VI
H Hôtel F1, 9, rue Périgot, ✆ 089/1705317, I-II
H Ibis Budget Metz-Est Technopole, 3, rue des Dinandiers, ✆ 089/2701255, II-III
H Ibis Cathédrale, 47, rue Chambière, ✆ 310173, III
H Ibis Gare, 3, bis rue Vauban, ✆ 219090, III-IV
H Kyriad Metz Centre, 8, rue du Père Potot, ✆ 365556, IV-V
H La Pergola, 13, route de Plappeville, ✆ 325294, III
H La Citadelle, 5, avenue Ney, ✆ 171717, VII
H Lutece, 11, rue de Paris, ✆ 302725, II
H Mercure, 29, place St. Thiébault, ✆ 385050, V
H Métropole, 5, place du Général de Gaulle, ✆ 662622, III-IV
H Metz-Technopole, 1, rue Félix Savart, ✆ 399450, VI-VII
H Moderne, 1, rue Lafayette, ✆ 665733, III-IV
H Novotel, Centre St. Jacques, ✆ 373839, V-VI

H Première Classe, Route d'Ars-Laquenexy, ✆ 089/2234898, II

H Terminus, 13, rue Lafayette, ✆ 87668118, I-III

BB L'aparté, Promenade Hildegarde, ✆ 068/1285445, V

BB Les chambres de l'île, rue de l'Horticulture, ✆ 373051, II-IV

🏠 Auberge de Jeunesse de Metz-Plage, 1, allée de Metz Plage, ✆ 304402

🏠 Auberge de Jeunesse Carrefour, 6, rue Marchant, ✆ 750726

⛺ Camping de Metz-Plage, Allée de Metz-Plage, ✆ 682648, I

Woippy (F) (L)

Postal code: 57140; Area code: 0387

ℹ Office de Tourisme, Place de l'Hôtel de Ville, ✆ 346300

H Campanile, 54, Rue du Fort Gambetta, ✆ 308383, IV-V

H Comfort Inn Primevère, Route de Thionville, ✆ 303003, IV

H Ibis Metz Nord, 56, Rue du Fort Gambetta, ✆ 342000, IV-V

La Maxe (F) (L)

Postal code: 57140; Area code: 0387

Pz Michel, 10, chemin derrière la Croix,

✆ 068/3284410, III-V

Rugy (F) (R)

Postal code: 57640; Area code: 0387

H La Bergerie, 10, rue de la Bergerie, ✆ 778227, V-VI

Hauconcourt (F) (L)

Postal code: 57280; Area code: 0387

H Novotel, ✆ 801818, V-VII

Ennery (F) (R)

Postal code: 57365; Area code: 0387

H Formule 1, 1 rue du Gay Lussac, ✆ 737302, III

Talange (F) (L)

Postal code: 57525; Area code: 0387

H du Triangle, rue des Allies, ✆ 711718, II

H La Tarentelle, Zone Actipôle, ✆ 722459, III-V

H Première Classe, 7, rue des Allies, ✆ 721311, III

Hagondange (F) (L)

Postal code: 57141; Area code: 0387

ℹ Office de Tourisme, Place Jean Burger, ✆ 703527

H du Centre, 7, rue Anatole France, ✆ 714764, II-V

Amnéville-les-Thermes (F) (L)

Postal code: 57360; Area code: 0387

ℹ Office de Tourisme, Rue du Bois de Coulange, ✆ 701040

H Amnéville Plaza, Parc du Bois de Coulange, ✆ 718286, VI-VII

H de la Maison d'Hôtes, Bois de Coulange, ✆ 401120,

III-V

H Diane, Rue de la Source, ✆ 701633, V

H Le Roi Soleil, Bois de Coulange, ✆ 401515, III

H Marso, Bois de Coulange, ✆ 151540, VI

H Orion, Rue des Thermes, ✆ 702020, V

H Saint-Eloy, Rue des Thermes, ✆ 703262, V

H Résidence Les Sources, Bois de Coulange, ✆ 708100

Thionville (F) (L)

Postal code: 57100; Area code: 0382

ℹ Office du Tourisme, 16, rue du Vieux Collège, ✆ 533318

H Best Western le Concorde, 6, place du Luxembourg, ✆ 340090, V-VI

H des Oliviers, 1 rue du Four-Banal, ✆ 537027, IV

H du Parc, 10, place de la République, ✆ 828080, III

H Domain de Volkrange, 50, rue du Donjon, ✆ 593800, V

H Foch, 69, boulevard Maréchal-Foch, ✆ 542827, V

H Kyriad Design Enzo, 96, Route de Buchel, ✆ 821007, IV-V

H Kyriad Prestige, 9, Allée Raymond Poincaré, ✆ 503467, V

H L'Horizon, 50 route du Crève-Coeur, ✆ 885365, VI

H Mercure Thionville Centre, 2, rue Georges-Dirsch, ✆ 518422, IV

H Sirius, 63, avenue Comte de Bertier, ✆ 548484, IV

🏠 Auberge de Jeunesse Thionville, 3 place de la Gare, ✆ 563214

⛺ Camping Municipal de Thionville, 6, rue du Parc, ✆ 538375

Yutz (F) (R)

Postal code: 57970; Area code: 0382

H Hotel F1 Thionville-Yutz, 1, rue des Carolingiens, ✆ 0891/1705405, II-III

H Ibis, 38, rue du Vieux Bourg, ✆ 866666, IV-V

H Ibis Budget Thionville-Yutz, 3, rue des Carolingiens, ✆ 089/2683217, III

Cattenom (F) (L)

Postal code: 57570; Area code: 0382

Pz Eberhardt, 34, rue Kennedy, ✆ 553639, II

Koenigsmacker (F) (R)

Postal code: 57970; Area code: 0382

H La Lorraine, 1 rue de L'Eglise, ✆ 503350, VI

Pz Keichinger, Moulin de Méwinckel, ✆ 552328, III

Malling (F) (R)

Postal code: 57480; Area code: 0382

⛺ Camping de Malling, 2, rue du Plan-d'Eau, ✆ 501297

Rettel (F) (R)

Postal code: 57480; Area code: 0382

⛺ Camping de Rettel, 15, rue de Contz, ✆ 837209

Sierck-les-Bains (F) (R)
Postal code: 57480; Area code: 0382
🛈 Office de Tourisme, Rue du Château, ☎ 837414
🏕 Camping de Sierck-les-Bains, Chemin des Tilleuls, ☎ 837239

Manderen (F) (R)
Postal code: 57480; Area code: 0382
H Au relais du Château Mensberg, 15, rue du château, ☎ 837316, V

Perl (R)
Postal code: 66706; Area code: 06867
🛈 Gemeindeverwaltung, Trierer Str. 28, ☎ 660
H Hammes, Hubertus-v.-Nell-Str. 15, ☎ 91030, V ◉
H Greiveldinger, Bergstr. 1-3, ☎ 271, V
H Hotel Struppshof, Struppshof 1, ☎ 06868/93140, III
H Alte Maimühle, Bahnhofstr. 100, ☎ 91131718, IV-V
H Perler Hof, Bergstr. 2-4, ☎ 561594, IV-V
H Sonnenhof, Eft-Hellendorf, Merziger Str. 3, ☎ 06868/773, IV ◉
Hg Residence garni, Hubertus-von-Nell-Str. 19, ☎ 911910, V
Gh Winandy, Biringer Str. 2, ☎ 364, IV
Pz Fiehn, Bahnhofstr. 11, ☎ 5247, II
Pz Görg, Bahnhofstr. 10, ☎ 5455, II
Pz Klein, Trierer Str. 13, ☎ 5205, II
Pz Klein, Bergstr. 12-14, ☎ 777, II

Pz Lamberti, Kirschenstr. 33, ☎ 5147, II
Pz Masseria-Rosa dei Venti, Am Dreiländereck 3, ☎ 910874, II
Pz Köck, Zur Kopp 9a, ☎ 5351, II
Pz Sinnwell-Sieren, Bergstr. 51, ☎ 444, II

Nennig (R)
Postal code: 66706; Area code: 06866
🛈 Tourist-Info Verkehrsverein Nennig, Bübinger Str. 5, ☎ 1439
H Victor`s Residenz-Hotel, Schlossstr. 27-29, ☎ 790, VII
H Zur Traube, Bübinger Str. 22, ☎ 349, V
H Zum Mosaik, Berger Weg 9, ☎ 151558, IV-VS
🏕 Mosella, Am Rothaus/Moselufer, ☎ 510
🏕 Dreiländereck, Sinzer Str. 1, ☎ 322

Schengen (Lux) (L)
Postal code: 5444; Area code: 00352
H Château de Schengen, 2 beim Schlass, ☎ 236638, VII ◉

Remerschen (Lux) (L)
Postal code: 5440; Area code: 00352
🏠 Jugendherberge Remerschen, 31 Wäistrooss, ☎ 2666731, III ◉

Schwebsange (Lux) (L)
Postal code: 5447; Area code: 00352
🏕 Camping du Port, Route Nationale 10,

☎ 26664460 ◉

Remich (Lux) (L)
Postal code: 5533; Area code: 00352
🛈 Syndicat d'Initiative et Tourisme Remich, 4 Rue Enz, ☎ 23698488
H St. Nicolas, 31 Esplanade, ☎ 26663, VII ◉
H Croisette, 4 Quai de la Moselle, ☎ 26660505, III
H des Cygnes, 11 Esplanade, ☎ 23698852, III
H de L'Esplanade, 5 Esplanade, ☎ 23669171, III-V
H des Vignes, 29 Route de Mondorf, ☎ 23699149, V
H Villa Belle-Rive, 49 route de Stadtbredimus, ☎ 27075677, V

Stadtbredimus (Lux) (L)
Postal code: 5450; Area code: 00352
H de l'Ecluse, 29 Wäistrooss, route du Vin, ☎ 2361911, VI ◉

Palzem (R)
Postal code: 54439; Area code: 06583
H Zur Moselterrasse, Bahnhofstr. 3, ☎ 610, III
H Rebenhof, Obermoselstr. 9, ☎ 537, III ◉
P Schloss Thorn, An der B 419, ☎ 433, III
P Weingut Brunnenhof, Römerstr. 14, ☎ 452, III ◉
Pz Sonnenberg, Römerstr. 2, ☎ 444, III
🏕 Opa Schuler, Obermoselstr. 1, ☎ 678

Ehnen (Lux) (L)
Postal code: 5417; Area code: 00352

Fw Distillerie Dolizy & Guillon, 5 Kiirchegaessel, ☎ 456706, VI ◉

Wormeldange (Lux) (L)
Postal code: 5480; Area code: 00352
H Relais du Postillon, 113 Rue Principale, ☎ 768485, IV

Wincheringen (R)
Postal code: 54457; Area code: 06583
H Moselblick, Am Mühlenberg 1, ☎ 99480, V

Rehlingen (R)
Postal code: 54453; Area code: 06583
H Moselblick, Bergstr. 6, ☎ 567, III
P Temmes, Am Haarberg 16, ☎ 310, II
Pz Biringer, Am Brunnen 3, ☎ 730, II
Pz Winzerhof Reiter, Am Haarberg 11, ☎ 289, III
Pz Weingut Weber-Temmes, Am Haarberg 24, ☎ 810, III

Nittel (R)
Postal code: 54453; Area code: 06584
🛈 Heimat- und Verkehrsverein, Weinstr. 42, ☎ 99360
P Weingut Sonntag, Kirchenweg 22, ☎ 7139, III ◉
H Hampshire Moselhotel Nitteler Hof, Weinstr. 42, ☎ 99360, V ◉
H Zum Mühlengarten, Uferstr. 5, ☎ 91420, IV-V
Gh Culinarium, Weinstr. 5, ☎ 91450, IV-V

Gh Holbach-Müller, Kirchenweg 15, ☎ 321, III

Gh Weingut Dostert-Schmitt, Kirchenweg 5, ☎ 7105, III

P Hellershof-Zilliken, Weinstr. 14, ☎ 91500, V

P Weingut Apel, Weinstr. 26, ☎ 314, IV-V

Pz Jürgen Dostert, Moselstr. 45, ☎ 263, III

Pz Weingut Dostert, Im Stolzenwingert 24, ☎ 7104, III

Pz Weingut Frieden, Uferstr. 4, ☎ 306, IV ◉

Wellen (R)
Postal code: 54441; Area code: 06584

Gh Pehna's Restaurant, Moselstr. 8, ☎ 91400, III

Temmels (R)
Postal code: 54441; Area code: 06584

Gh Zur Mosel, Moselstr. 2, ☎ 347, III

Grevenmacher (Lux) (L)
Postal code: 6776; Area code: 00352

H Simon's Plaza, 7 Potashberg, ☎ 267444

⛺ Grevenmacher Camping, ☎ Route du Vin, ☎ 750234

Mertert (Lux) (L)
Postal code: 6674; Area code: 00352

H Goedert, 4 Place de la Gare, ☎ 740021

Wasserbillig (Lux) (L)
Postal code: 6633; Area code: 00352

H Kinnen, 32 route de Luxembourg, ☎ 740088, III-IV

Langsur (L)
Postal code: 54308; Area code: 06501

ℹ Deutsch-Luxemb. Tourist Information, Moselstr. 1, ☎ 602666

H Löwener Mühle Da Capris, Moselstr. 36, ☎ 608031, III-V

H Langsurer Mühle, Wasserbilliger Str. 5, ☎ 94010, III-IV

Mesenich
Pz Weingut Johannishof, Trierer Str. 24, ☎ 923390, II-III ◉

Oberbillig (R)
Postal code:54331; Area code: 06501

Gh Haus der Fischerei, Moselstr. 45, ☎ 9698730, III

Wasserliesch (R)
Postal code: 54332; Area code: 06501

P Weingut Giwer-Greif, Neudorfstr. 24, ☎ 180522, IV ◉

H Scheid's Hotel-Restaurant, Reinigerstr. 48, ☎ 9209792, V

H Albachmühle, Albach 6, ☎ 94950, III-IV ◉

Pz Landhaus Lutz, Römerstr. 62, ☎ 12349, III-IV

Pz Gästehaus Merges, Brunnenstr. 9, ☎ 14659, II

Pz Rausch, Hadelsgraben 9, ☎ 14877, II

Pz Haus Schuh, Im Kestenbüsch 1, ☎ 14860, II

Konz (R)
Postal code: 54329; Area code: 06501

ℹ Saar-Obermosel-Touristik e.V., Granastr. 22, ☎ 6018040

H Mühlentaler's Park Hotel, Granastr. 26, ☎ 2157, V

H Alt Conz, Gartenstr. 8, ☎ 93670 V ◉

H Schmidt-Lieblang, Bahnhofstr. 24, ☎ 3199, IV

Hg Schons, Merzlicher Str. 6-8, ☎ 9698355, III

P Luy, Am Berendsborn 20, ☎ 99404, III

Pz Campingplatz Konz, Am Moselufer 1 ☎ 2577, II

Pz Meiser, Fasanenweg 6, ☎ 5490, II

Pz Weiss, Wiltinger Str. 102, ☎ 7260, II

Pz Haus am Saarufer, Saarstr. 12, ☎ 600449, III

⛺ Campingplatz Konz, Am Moselufer 1 ☎ 2577

Könen
Pz Hettinger, Auf Tommet 19, ☎ 17821, II

⛺ Campingplatz Horsch, Könener Str. 36, ☎ 17571

Niedermennig/Tälchen
P Allegra Restaurant, Wendelinstr. 5, ☎ 946064, V

P Haus Heidi, Jakobstr. 9, ☎ 14012, II

Obermennig/Tälchen
H Eucharisberg, Am Großschock 7, ☎ 13362, IV

Tawern
Postal code: 54456; Area code: 06501

P Gorges, Kapellenstr. 30, ☎ 602052, II

P Scheidt, Römerstr. 40, ☎ 17824, II

Igel (L)
Postal code: 54308; Area code: 06501

ℹ Ferienregion Trierer Land e.V., Moselstr. 1, 54308 Langsur-Wasserbilligerbrück, ☎ 602666

H Igeler Säule, Trierer Str. 41, ☎ 92610, IV-V ◉

Pz Monzel, Trierer Str. 101, ☎ 16182, II

⛺ Igeler Säule, in der Nähe des Sportplatzes, ☎ 12944

Trier-Zewen (L)
Postal code: 54294; Area code: 0651

H Kugel, Kirchenstr. 17, ☎ 827730, II-III ◉

H Rebenhof, Wasserbilliger Str. 34, ☎ 827170, II-III

H Ambiente, In der Acht 1-2, ☎ 827280, V ◉

H Zewener Hof, Kantstr. 4, ☎ 8267700, III

P Scalla, Wasserbilliger Str. 32, ☎ 86441, II

Trier
Postal code: 54290; Area code: 0651

ℹ Tourist-Information Trier Stadt und Land e.V., An der Porta Nigra, ☎ 978080

H Astoria, Bruchhausener Str. 4, ☎ 97835-0, V

H Weinhaus Haag, Stockpl. 1 ☎ 975750

H Residenz Hotel Am Zuckerberg, Frauenstr. 7, ☎ 9793-0, IV-V ◉

H Mercure Porta Nigra, 54292, Porta-Nigra-Pl. 1, ☎ 2701-0, VI-VII

H Casa Verde, Hermeskeiler Str. 1, ☏ 9954-300, IV-V

H Park Plaza, Nikolaus-Koch-Pl. 1, ☏ 99930, VII

H Arcadia Hotel, 54295, Metzer Allee 6, ☏ 9377-0, V-VI

H Römischer Kaiser, 54292, Am Porta-Nigra-Pl. 6, ☏ 9770-100, VI

H Zum Christophel, An der Porta Nigra, ☏ 9794200, V

H Cityhotel Primavera, Johannisstr. 16, ☏ 1455250, IV-V ◉

H Penta Hotel, Kaiserstr. 29, ☏ 9495-0, V-VII

H Aulmann, Fleischstr. 47-48, ☏ 97670, V-VI

H Blesius Garten, 54295, Olewiger Str. 135, ☏ 36060, VI-VII ◉

H Nells Park, 54292, Dasbachstr. 12, ☏ 14440, V-VI

H Altstadthotel, Am Porta-Nigra-Platz, ☏ 9770200, VI

H Römerbrücke, 54294, Aachener Str. 5, ☏ 82660, V ◉

H Villa Hügel, 54295, Bernhardstr. 14, ☏ 33066, VI-VII

H Petrisberg, 54296, Sickingerstr. 11-13, ☏ 4640, V

H Feilen-Wolff, 54294, Kölner Str. 22, ☏ 87001, IV-V

H Alte Villa, Saarstr. 133, ☏ 938120, V-VII ◉

H Ehranger Hof, 54293, Ehranger Str. 207, ☏ 66111, IV ◉

H Pieper, 54292, Thebäerstr. 39, ☏ 23008, IV-V ◉

H Becker's, 54295, Olewiger Str. 206, ☏ 938080, V-VII

H Am Ufer, 54292, Zurmaiener Str. 81-83, ☏ 1453970, V

H Frankenturm, Dietrichstr. 3, ☏ 978240, V

H Warsberger Hof, Dietrichstr. 42, ☏ 975250, II

Hg Kessler, Brückenstr. 23, ☏ 978170, V-IV

Hg Paulin, 54292, Pauliner Str. 13, ☏ 147400, V-VI

Hg Casa Chiara, 54292, Engelstr. 8, ☏ 270730, V-VI

Hg Deutschherrenhof, Deutschherrenstr. 32, ☏ 975420, V

Hg Grund, 54292, Paulinstr. 7, ☏ 25939, IV-V

P Rosi, Turmstr. 14, ☏ 87085, III-IV

🏠 Gästehaus Eruopäische Akademie, 54292, Herzogenbuscher Str. 56, ☏ 146800, III

🏠 Hilles Hostel, 54295, Gartenfeldstr. 7, ☏ 7102785 ◉

🏠 Römerstadt Jugendherberge, 54292, An der Jugendherberge 4, ☏ 146620 ◉

🏠 Warsberger Hof, Dietrichstr. 42, ☏ 975250, II

🏠 Jugendsportheim Waldstadion, Kockelsberger Weg 21, ☏ 86663

🏕 Camping- und Reisemobilpark Treviris, 54294, Luxemburger Str. 81, ☏ 8200911

Euren

Postal code: 54294; Area code: 0651

H Haus Marianne, Eurener Str. 190a, ☏ 810040, III

H Eurener Hof, Eurener Str. 171, ☏ 82400, V-VI

Hg Schütz, Udostr. 74, ☏ 88838, III-IV

Pfalzel (L)

Postal code: 54293; Area code: 0651

H Klosterschenke, Klosterstr. 10, ☏ 968440, V ◉

Ruwer (R)

Postal code: 54292; Area code: 0651

H Zur Post, Ruwerer Str. 18, ☏ 5100, V-VI

Kasel

Postal code: 54317; Vorwahl. 0651

🛈 Tourist-Information Ruwer, Bahnhofstr. 37a, ☏ 1701818

Gh Pauliner Hof, Bahnhofstr. 41, ☏ 9679090, V

Gh Haus der Ruwer, Bahnhofstr. 3, ☏ 9950435, III-IV

Waldrach

Postal code: 54320; Area code: 06500

H Simon, Bahnhofstr. 14, ☏ 677, V

H Café Lichtenthal, Hermeskeiler Str. 42, ☏ 370, III

Kordel (L)

Postal code: 54306; Area code: 06505

🛈 Ferienregion Trierer Land e.V., Moselstr. 1, 54308 Langsur-Wasserbilligerbrück, ☏ 06501/602666

H Burg Ramstein, ☏ 1735, III-IV

H Neyses, Am Kreuzfeld 1, ☏ 91400, IV ◉

Hg Waldhotel Weis, Burg Ramstein, ☏ 359, III-IV

P Reichert, Hauptstr. 19-20, ☏ 1757, II-III

P Schneider, Edenstr. 4, ☏ 721, II ◉

Pz Weber, Hochmark 4, ☏ 910277, II

Kenn (R)

Postal code: 54344; Area code: 06502

H Waldfrieden, Vogelskopf 2-3, ☏ 5548, III

Gh Fröhliches Weinfass, Hauptstr. 1, ☏ 8435, III-IV ◉

P Kenner Treff, Bahnhofstr. 42, ☏ 9308737, III

Schweich (L)

Postal code: 54338; Area code: 06502

🛈 Tourist-Information Römische Weinstrasse, Brückenstr. 46, ☏ 93380

H Zum Stern, Brückenstr. 60, ☏ 910020, IV ◉

H Leinenhof, Leinenhof 5, ☏ 91860, IV

H Zur Moselbrücke, Brückenstr. 1, ☏ 91900, V

H Grefen, Brückenstr. 31, ☏ 92400, III-V

H Schweicher Hof, Brückenstr. 45, ☏ V

Hg Wagner, Langgartenstr. 25, ☏ 92090, III

Gh Isseler Hof, Isseler Hof 19, ☏ 8260, III

P Weingut Wallerath, Bahnhofstr. 25, ☏ 5554, II ◉

🏕 u. Restaurant Zum Fährturm, ☏ 91300

Longuich (R)

Postal code: 54340; Area code: 06502

🛈 Tourist-Information Römische Weinstrasse Longuich-Kirsch, Maximinstr. 18, ☏ 1716

P Restaurant Wein im Turm, Weinstr. 23, ☏ 5595, IV

◎

H Zur Linde, Cerisiersstr. 10, ✆ 5582, III

Gh Ferienweingut Jung, Raiffeisenstr. 10, ✆ 8619, III

P Weingut Franziskus-Hof, Cerisiersstr. 3, ✆ 91450, III ◎

P Alte Burg, Maximinstr. 39, ✆ 5587, III

P Thul-Hoff, Maximinstr. 5, ✆ 8302, II-III

P Zum Moselufer, Moselstr. 3, ✆ 5546, II

P Scholerhof, Tränkg. 6, ✆ 1621, II

P Schmitt-Bläsius, Freihof 2, ✆ 2685, II ◎

P Sorgen, Tränkg. 4, ✆ 5751, II

P Zentius, Im Freihof 8, ✆ 1216, II

P Sonntag, Hetzerothsgarten 1, ✆ 3622, II

Riol (R)

Postal code: 54340; Area code: 06502

ℹ Heimat- und Verkehrsverein Riol, Hauptstr. 13, ✆ 995546

P Weingut Weich, Bahnhofstr. 17, ✆ 2648, III ◎

H Triolago, Zur Talstation 1, ✆ 937460, IV

Gh Weingut Reichertshof, Hauptstr. 19, ✆ 7795, II-III

Gh Weingut Johanneshof, Hauptstr. 4, ✆ 54340

⛺ Waldsee, Moselstr. 13, ✆ 995560 u. 6421

Mehring (L)

Postal code: 54346; Area code: 06502

ℹ Touristinformation Mehring, Bachstr. 47, ✆ 1413

P Weingut Hoffranzen, Schulstr. 22, ✆ 8441, III

H Weingut Weiler, Moselstr. 9, ✆ 2237, III-IV

H Weinhaus Bernarda, Maximinstr. 7, ✆ 2788, IV

H Zum Moseltal, Peter-Schroeder-Pl. 1, ✆ 2656, III ◎

H Zum Fährturm, Peter Schroeder Pl. 2, ✆ 2403, III

Hg Haus am Fluss Im Bungert 12, ✆ 5017, V-VII ◎

Gh Zur Römervilla, Im Hostert 14, ✆ 4462, II-III

Gh Müller, Bachstr. 35, ✆ 99123, III

Gh Sebastiani, Neustr. 10, ✆ 1000, III

Gh Zum Kellerstübchen, Deierbachstr. 9, ✆ 2709, III ◎

Gh Alt Mehring, Linterstr. 3, ✆ 931950, III ◎

P Loskill, Am Rebenhang 2, ✆ 2817, II

P Basten-Olinger, Im Ganggarten 20, ✆ 2895, II

P Rebenblick, Weinbergstr. 14, ✆ 5862, I-II

P Heimfahrt-Wagner, Medardusstr. 26, ✆ 7698, II

P Weingut Reis, Im Bungert 8, ✆ 2529, III

P Schroeder, Bachstr. 13a, ✆ 3682, II

P Dixius, In Lörsch 23, ✆ 2254, II

P Marianne Bach, Gartenstr. 1, ✆ 5637, II

P Winzerhof Reis-Kohl, Im Bungert 3a, ✆ 8773, III

⛺ Campingplatz Mehring, ✆ 7612

Pölich (L)

Postal code: 54340; Area code: 06507

P Schömann, Hauptstr. 4, ✆ 3193, II

H Pölicher Held, Hauptstr. 5, ✆ 93600, II-III

P Huchler, Olkenstr. 16, ✆ 3083, II

⛺ Campingplatz zur Pölicher Held, Im Winkel 6, ✆ 3475

⛺ Campingplatz Moselherz, ✆ 4205

⛺ Moselcamping „Pölicher Held", Am Sportplatz, ✆ 703347

Schleich (L)

Postal code: 54340; Area code: 06507

Gh Drockenmüller, Kapellenstr. 5, ✆ 3748, I-II

Gh Ferienweingut Scholer, Moselweinstr. 17, ✆ 3151, II-III

P Winzerhof Schiefergold, Kapellenstr. 9, ✆ 3335, II

P Weingut Rummel, Weierbachstr. 8, ✆ 3282, II

P Otto, Am Kraftwerk 4, ✆ 3459, II

P Scholer, Im Kardel 6, ✆ 3710, II

Detzem (R)

Postal code: 54340; Area code: 06507

H Zum Anker, Ankerstr. 3, ✆ 3354, II

Gh Gästehaus Dorothea, Neugartenstr. 7, ✆ 3147, II ◎

P Weingut Thömmes, Bahnhofstr. 13, ✆ 3701, I-II

P Steffes, Bahnhofstr. 2, ✆ 3880, II

P Porten, Bahnhofstr. 8, ✆ 8100, II

Pz Merges, Hauptstr. 25, ✆ 3423, II

Pz Steffes-Basten, Hauptstr. 4, ✆ 3585, II

Pz Weingut Schmitz, Neustr. 15, ✆ 3401, II

Pz Regneri, Neustr. 14, ✆ 3616, II

Pz Mander, Olkstr. 6, ✆ 3561, II

Pz Weingut Dany-Winnebeck, Maximinerstr. 4, ✆ 3544, II

Thörnich (R)

Postal code: 54340; Area code: 06507

P Winzerhof Thimmel, Hauptstr. 15, ✆ 3742, II ◎

P Schmitt-Hof, Detzemer Weg 10, ✆ 3206, IV-V

P Longen, Hauptstr. 6, ✆ 3339, II

P Thul, Im Bungert 6, ✆ 3752, II ◎

Pz Linden, Hauptstr. 25, ✆ 3187, II

Ensch (L)

Postal code: 54340; Area code: 06507

H Breidbach, Martinstr. 9, ✆ 939466, III

Gh Ferienweingut St. Martin, Martinstr. 16, ✆ 4220, III

Klüsserath (L)

Postal code: 54340; Area code: 06507

H Zum Rebstock, Salmstr. 8, ✆ 93510, III

P Weingut Jostock-Lex, Hauptstr. 127, ✆ 4500, II

P Blesius-Wagner, Mittelstr. 81, ✆ 4610, II

Pz Berweiler, Mittelstr. 109, ✆ 993242, III

Pz Scholtes, Hauptstr. 168, ✆ 4286, II

Pz Herres, Hauptstr. 117, ✆ 99123, II-III

Pz Lex, Mittelstr. 5, ✆ 4689, II

Pz Lex-Welter, Hauptstr. 132, ✆ 4594, II

Pz Regnery, Burgweg 2, ☏ 4585, II

Pz Zur alten Salmbrücke, Hauptstr. 3, ☏ 4633, II

⛺ Campingplatz Moselblick, ☏ 4667

Köwerich (R)

Postal code: 54340; Area code: 06507

H Moselhotel Ludwigs, Beethovenstr. 14, ☏ 802456, IV 📶

Gh Weingut-Gästehaus Porten-Becker, Beethovenstr. 45, ☏ 3786, II 📶

Pz Klären, Beethovenstr. 40, ☏ 3787, II

Leiwen (R)

Postal code: 54340; Area code: 06507

P Weingut Scholtes, Schulstr. 5, ☏ 3822, III

H Zummethof, Panoramaweg 1-3, ☏ 93550, IV-V

H Weinhaus Weis, Römerstr. 10, ☏ 93610, III-IV 📶

H Schu, Mühlenstr. 4, ☏ 3118, III

H „Alte Metzgerei" Herres, Römerstr. 11, ☏ 3328, III-V

Hg Hof Sonnental, Schulstr. 19, ☏ 3242, II-III

Gh Sektstuuf „St. Laurentius", Euchariusstr. 15, ☏ 939055, V

Gh Löwenhof, Flurgartenstr. 2m ☏ 3598, III

P Jostock-Hermes, Maximinstr. 17, ☏ 3156, III-IV

P Lex-Ambré, Matthiasstr. 16, ☏ 3202, II-III

P Porten, Am Sportpl. 5, ☏ 3366, II

P Alexanderhof, Liviastr. 24, ☏ 4314, II-III

P Weingut Loersch, Tannenweg 11, ☏ 3229, III-IV

P Steffes, Matthiasstr. 22, ☏ 3520, II-III

P Klostergarten, Stefanusstr. 6, ☏ 3523, II-III

P Spieles, Schulstr. 20, ☏ 2787, II

P Kurtrier Hof, Tränkg. 4, ☏ 3025, II

P Scholtes, Schulstr. 1, ☏ 8338, II

P Haus Mosella, Tannenweg 17, ☏ 3532, II-III

P Livia, Flurgartenstr. 5, ☏ 3623, II-III

Pz Löwen, Klostergartenstr. 8, ☏ 4728, II

Pz Feller-Porten, Matthiasstr. 23, ☏ 3569, III-IV

Fw St. Maximin, Maximinstr. 15, ☏ 802060, III

⛺ Campingplatz Landal Green Parks, Sonnenberg, ☏ 93690

Trittenheim (L)

Postal code: 54349; Area code: 06507

ℹ️ Tourist-Information, Moselweinstr. 55, ☏ 2227

H Gutshotel Galerie Riesling, Moselweinstr. 42, ☏ 939774, V

H Krone-Riesling, Moselpromenade 9, ☏ 92630, V

Hg Clüsserath-Weiler, An der Brücke, ☏ 5011, III-IV

Gh Weinstube „Essen beim Winzer", Moselweinstr. 40, ☏ 5584, III

Gh Weingut-Gästehaus Bernhard Eifel, Laurentiusstr. 17, ☏ 5972, III-IV 📶

P Clüsserath, Moselweinstr. 67, ☏ 701853, II-III

Pz Weingut Arenz, Olkstr. 16, ☏ 5175, III

Pz Weingut Arenz-Lorenz, Moselweinstr. 7, ☏ 5212, II

Pz Gästehaus Basten, Joh.-Trithemiusstr. 7, ☏ 5626, II-III

Pz Hermeshof, Ettenstr. 21, ☏ 5380, III-IV

Pz Spieleshof, Spielesstr. 5, ☏ 2639, II-III

Pz Gästehaus Hermes, Brückenstr. 1, ☏ 5004, III-IV

Pz Weingut Clüsserath, Im Hof 7, ☏ 2167, II-III

Pz Weingut Lukashof, Moselweinstr. 86, ☏ 2031, II-III

Pz Maringer, Olkstr. 1, ☏ 2520, III

Pz Boch, Moselweinstr. 62, ☏ 2713, III

Pz Weingut Bollig, Am Kreuzweg 3, ☏ 5346, II

Pz Bollig, Olkstr. 20, ☏ 6231, II-III 📶

Pz Britz, Im Hof 3, ☏ 2538, II-III

Pz Weingut Clüsserath, Moselpromenade, ☏ 992121, III

Pz Hubertushof, Moselweinstr. 13, ☏ 7124, II 📶

Pz Gästehaus Sigrid, Brückenstr. 2, ☏ 5746, III

Pz Weingut Eifel-Zimmer, Engelbert-Schue-Weg 2, ☏ 5089, II-III

Pz Weingut Hermen, Joh.-Trithemiusstr. 59, ☏ 70016, III-IV

Pz Weinstube Hermes-Granz, Moselweinstr. 40, ☏ 5584, II-III

Pz Weingut Hermes-Lex, Moselweinstr. 2, ☏ 5388, II

Pz Weingut Hoffmann, Ergenesschstr. 17, ☏ 5316, III

Pz Hoffmann, Moselweinstr. 72, ☏ 2521, III

Pz Weingut Kuhnen, Auf dem Spieles 1-3, ☏ 2689, II

Pz Weingut Lentes, Ettenstr. 5, ☏ 2517, II 📶

Pz Weingut Maringer, Am Kreuzweg 4, ☏ 2532, II

Pz Weingut Maringer-Bollig, Clemensstr. 29, ☏ 2720, II-III

Pz Weingut Monzel, Im Weingarten 5, ☏ 6141, II

Pz Weingut Schmitt, Moselstr. 27, ☏ 2527, III 📶

Pz Weingut Scholtes-Kirsten, Moselpromenade 17, ☏ 2437, II

Pz Gästehaus Scholtes-Hammes, Moselweinstr. 90, ☏ 2716, II-III

Pz Weingut Scholtes, Im Gospert 14, ☏ 6472, II

Pz Weingut Steffen, Olkstr. 9, ☏ 2276, II

⛺ Campingplatz „Im Grünen", Olkstr. 12, ☏ 2148

Neumagen (R)

Postal code: 54347; Area code: 06507

ℹ️ Verkehrsbüro, Hinterburg 8a, ☏ 6555

H Römerweinschiff, Römerstr. 123, ☏ 2188, III-IV

H Zur Post, Römerstr. 9, ☏ 939771, IV

H Zum Anker, Moselstr. 14, ☏ 6397, IV-V 📶

H Haus Wittgenstein, Grafenweg 1, ☏ 0177/4932822, III-IV

H Zum Dhrontal, Harpelsteinstr. 15, ☏ 3112, II-III

Gh Reiterhof Kron, Kronberg, ☏ 3477, II

Gh Weingut Konstantinhöhe, Konstantinhöhe, ☏ 2168, II 📶

P Haus Berghof, Bergstr. 10, ☏ 2108, III-IV

P Warsberger Weinhof, Römerstr. 98, ✆ 92580, III-IV

Pz Weingut Bollig, St. Helenastr. 16, ✆ 5883, II

Pz Weingut C. Lemmermeyer, Spielesstr. 18, ✆ 2397, II

Pz Bollig, Römerstr. 32, ✆ 5253, II

Pz Everz, Bulchinstr. 9, ✆ 2823, III

Pz Weingut Lemmermeyer, Römerstr. 1, ✆ 2571, II

Pz Weingut Philipps, Weingartenstr. 16, ✆ 5744, III

Pz Schmitz, Im Lampertsgarten 8, ✆ 5844, II

Dhron (R)

Postal code: 54347; Area code: 06507

H Zum Hofberg, Brückenstr. 3, ✆ 2595, III

P Weinschröterhof, Metschert 39-41, ✆ 5340, II-III

Pz Kohl, Im Folz 24, ✆ 5742, II

Pz Spieles, Im Wiesental 14a, ✆ 5173, III

Pz Schneider, Im Weinberg 27, ✆ 5371, II

⛺ Neumagen-Dhron, Moselstr. 100, ✆ 5249

Piesport (L)

Postal code: 54498; Area code: 06507

ℹ Tourist-Information, Heinrich-Schmitt-Pl. 1, ✆ 2027

H Piesporter Goldtröpfchen, Am Domhof 5, ✆ 2442, III-V

Pz Kettern, Müsterterstr. 14, ✆ 2813, III-IV

Pz Weingut Birkenhof, Ketterg. 14, ✆ 2403, III 📷

Pz Weingut Lehnert Veit, In der Dur 10, ✆ 2123, III-IV 📷

H Haus Moselblick, Moselstr. 20, ✆ 2421, IV-V

H Moselloreley, Moselstr. 16, ✆ 2473, III

H Zum Römerbrunnen, Am Römerbrunnen 13, ✆ 992017, II-III

H Moselpanorama, Am Berg 1, ✆ 5130, III-V

Hg Winzerhof, Bahnhofstr. 8a, ✆ 92520, V

Gh Alt Piesport, Ausoniusufer 1, ✆ 6506, III-IV

P Freundenreich, Kirchpl. 22, ✆ 2691, II-III

P Weinhaus Alt Reinsport, Moselstr. 4, ✆ 2396, III-IV

P Bäckerei Kettern, Steing. 22, ✆ 2479, II

Pz Basten, Römerstr. 46, ✆ 5294, II

Pz Britz, Auf der Kaub 43, ✆ 5596, II

Pz Bujung, Schulstr. 8, ✆ 5652, II

Pz Ebert-Neukirch, Weingartenstr. 19, ✆ 6391, II

Pz Esseln, Auf der Kaub 27, ✆ 2162, II

Pz Franzen, Bernkasteler Str. 3, ✆ 2486, II

Pz Lenhardt, Brotstr. 20, ✆ 2845, II

Pz Gästehaus Kirsten, Loreleyblick 6, ✆ 2557, II

Pz Lehnert-Später, Brückenstr. 21, ✆ 99063, III

Pz Mertes-Lorenz, Pützbungert 11, ✆ 5808, II

Pz Weingut St. Joseph, In der Dur 11, ✆ 5161, II 📷

Pz Weller-Veit, St. Michaelstr. 26, ✆ 2315, II

Pz Weingut Weller-Lehnert, St. Michaelstr. 29, ✆ 2498, II-III

Pz Karthäuserhof, Karthäuserpl. 8, ✆ 5449, III-IV

Pz Pauly, Loreleyblick 1, ✆ 2771, II

Minheim (L)

Postal code: 54518; Area code: 06507

Gh Zur Brücke, In der Olk 10, ✆ 5810, II

Pz Weinbau Rößler, Klausener Str. 15, ✆ 2800, II 📷

Pz Weingut Brunnenhof, In der Kordel 2, ✆ 992006, II-III 📷

Pz Weingut Hoffmann, Moselweinstr. 14, ✆ 992090, II

Pz Weingut Thielen-Schunk & Sohn, In der Kordel 12, ✆ 6190, II-III 📷

Pz Koenen, Moselweinstr. 41 ✆ 99055, II

P Weingut Zisch, Am Eichhaus 2a, ✆ 5007, II 📷

Wintrich (R)

Postal code: 54487; Area code: 06534

ℹ Tourist-Information, Bergstr. 3, ✆ 8628

H Weinhaus Simon, Am Martiergarten 3, ✆ 664, IV

P Matthiashof, Bergstr. 12/13, ✆ 93250, II

H Moselblick, Bergstr. 42, ✆ 621, II-III 📷

H Wendland, Rosenstr. 12, ✆ 8796, II

Gh Im Brühl, Moselstr. 16, ✆ 405, II-III

P Weingut Thömmes, Kurfürstenstr. 21, ✆ 503, II 📷

P Martinerhof, Moselweinstr. 84, ✆ 426, II

P Arens-Föhr, Moselweinstr. 86, ✆ 782, II

Pz Haus Linden-Pelzer, Moselweinstr. 7, ✆ 8696, I-II

Pz Lorenz, Römerstr. 11, ✆ 677, II 📷

Brauneberg (R)

Postal code: 54472; Area code: 06534

H Weingutshotel Kohl, Moselweinstr. 48, ✆ 633, IV-V

H Brauneberger Hof, Moselweinstr. 136, ✆ 1400, V

H Weinhaus Schneider, Moselweinstr. 193, ✆ 8811, III

H Zur Grafschaft, Moselweinstr. 130, ✆ 322, II-III

P Moselblick, Lindenstr. 6-8, ✆ 8687, I-II

Pz Weingut Leo Erz-Baum, Kirchg. 10, ✆ 293, II 📷

Mülheim (R)

Postal code: 54486; Area code: 06534

H Domizil Schiffmann, Hauptstr. 52, ✆ 947690, V

H Zur Post, Hauptstr. 65, ✆ 93920, IV

P Gästehaus Caspary, Sonnenlayweg 5, ✆ 8202, II

P Weingut & Gästehaus Bottler, Hauptstr. 11, ✆ 324, II

Maring-Noviand

Postal code: 54484; Vorwahl. 06535

P Fries, Zum Brauneberg 16, ✆ 493, IV

Pz Römerpfad, In der Duhr 11, ✆ 7357

Pz Weingut Schmitt, Moselstr. 27, ✆ 563, IV 📷

Lieser (L)

Postal code: 54470; Area code: 06531

P Landhaus Kuntz, Schlossbergstr. 23, ✆ 3875, II-III 📷

H Steffen, Moselstr. 2, ✆ 9570, IV-V

H Schlosshotel Raatz, Moselstr. 44, ☎ 971830, IV
H Weinhaus Stettler, Moselstr. 41, ☎ 7550, III
P Löwen-Herges, Beethovenstr. 3, ☎ 3322, III-IV

Andel (R)

Postal code: 54470; Area code: 06531

P Feriengut Bohn, Goldbachstr. 7, ☎ 8443, III ◉
Gh Rosi, Goldbachstr. 37, ☎ 6346, II

Bernkastel-Kues

Postal code: 54470; Area code: 06531

🛈 Mosellandtouristik GmbH, Kordelweg 1 (Andel), ☎ 97330
🛈 Mosel-Gäste-Zentrum, Gestade 6 (Bernkastel), ☎ 500190

Bernkastel (R)

H Zur Post, Gestade 17, ☎ 96700, V
H Burg Landshut, Gestade 11, ☎ 3019, III-VI
H Bären, Schanzstr. 9, ☎ 950440, V-VI
H Moselblümchen, Schwanenstr. 10, ☎ 2335, IV-V
H Doctor-Weinstube, Hebeg. 5, ☎ 96650, V-VI ◉
H Binz, Markt 1, ☎ 2225, IV-V ◉
H Bernkasteler Hof, Hebeg. 1, ☎ 3218, III-V
H Burkard, Burgstr. 1, ☎ 2380, III-IV
H Märchenhotel, Kallenfelsstr. 25-27, ☎ 96550, VII
H Vital- und Wellnesshotel Zum Kurfürsten, Amsel-weg 1, ☎ 96770, IV-VI ◉
Hg Haus Weiskopf, Karlstr. 14, ☎ 2351, III-V
Hg Alter Posthof, Burgstr. 26, ☎ 91257, III-IV

Gh Kapuzinerstübchen, Römerstr. 35, ☎ 2353, III
P Gästehaus am Schloßberg, Burgstr. 18, ☎ 6572, II-IV
Pz Haus Bonsai, Burgstr. 53, ☎ 7728, II-III
Pz Dahm, Burgstr. 89, ☎ 8166, II

Kues (L)

H Drei Könige, Bahnhofstr. 1, ☎ 2035, V
H Alt-Kues, Nikolausufer 48, ☎ 2533, III
H Rosi, Nikolausufer 26, ☎ 6433, III-IV
H Christiana's Wein & Art Hotel, Lindenweg 18, ☎ 6627, III-IV ◉
H Burgblickhotel, Goethestr. 29, ☎ 922770, III
H Ristorante Spinelli, Bahnhofstr. 11, ☎ 2436, II-III
H Hoffmanns Weinstube, Bahnhofstr. 6, ☎ 2575, III
Hg Haus Anja, Bergweg 5b, ☎ 6178, III-IV
Hg Carola, Birkenweg 3, ☎ 4044, II-III
Hg Panorama, Rebschulweg 48, ☎ 3061, III-V ◉
Hg Weinhaus Arns, Jugendheimstr. 1, ☎ 6825, II-III
P Haus Irene, Lindenweg 6, ☎ 8261, III
P Weingut Hauth, Balduinstr. 1, ☎ 2294, III-IV
P Gästehaus Mertz, Am Weinberg, Raustr. 19, ☎ 6394, II
P Geller, Birkenweg 1, ☎ 6536, II-III
P Schwab, Weingartenstr. 56-58, ☎ 8043, II
P Haus Edeltrud, Nikolausufer 35, ☎ 6584, II-III
P Port, Weingartenstr. 57, ☎ 91173, II-III ◉

P Haus Lotti, Brüningstr. 12/14, ☎ 6565, II-III
P Haus Coen, Im Viertheil 2, ☎ 8186, II-III
Pz Haus Bartz, Im Altenwald 34, ☎ 6896, I-II
Pz Haas-Herges, Jugendheimstr. 11, ☎ 6494, II
Pz Hettgen, Cusanusstr. 25, ☎ 6125, II
Pz Rosemarie, Im Weierfeld 44, ☎ 6894, II
Pz Vianden, Schützenweg 10, ☎ 2797, I-II
Pz Robbecke, Friedrichstr. 11, ☎ 2488
🏠 Jugendherberge, Nähe Burgr. Landshut, ☎ 2395 ◉
🏕 Campingpl. Kueser Werth, ☎ 8200

Graach (R)

Postal code: 54470; Area code: 06531

🛈 Verkehrsbüro, Hauptstr. 94, ☎ 2541
H Zum Josefshof, Hauptstr. 128, ☎ 2272, III
H Kemmer´s Panorama Hotel, Panoramastr. 12, ☎ 4505, III
H Weinhaus Pfeiffer, Gestade 12, ☎ 96350, III-IV
P Winzerwirtschaft Philipps-Eckstein, Panoramastr. 11, Schäferei, ☎ 6542, III
P Weingut Petrushof, Weingartenstr. 20, ☎ 8594, II-III

Wehlen (L)

Postal code: 54470; Area code: 06531

H Mosel-Hotel, Uferallee 3, ☎ 97170, IV-V
H Sonnenlay, Fischerstr. 1, ☎ 6496, III-V

H Landhaus Ruth, Hauptstr. 169, ☎ 96110, IV
H Moselblick, Hauptstr. 2, ☎ 6262, II-III
H Hauth, Hauptstr. 109, ☎ 8424, II-III
H Moselbrücke, Brückenstr. 26, ☎ 96360, III
Gh Zum Weierborn, Hauptstr. 115, ☎ 8420, III
P Prüm, Uferallee 25, ☎ 3110, IV-V
Pz Otto´s Fahrradherberge, Hauptstr. 58, ☎ 973257, II ◉
🏕 Campingplatz Schenk, Hauptstr. 165, ☎ 8176

Zeltingen-Rachtig (R)

Postal code: 54492; Area code: 06532

🛈 Verkehrsbüro, Uferallee 13, ☎ 2404
H Deutschherrenhof, Deutschherrenstr. 23, ☎ 9350, V
H St. Stephanus, Uferallee 9, ☎ 680, VI-VII
H Nicolay Zur Post, Uferallee 7, ☎ 93910, V
H Winzerverein, Burgstr. 7, ☎ 2321, IV-VI
H Moselblick, Uferallee 20, ☎ 2343, III
H Chur Köln, Deutschherrenstr. 17, ☎ 9518940, III-V
H Zeltinger Hof, Kurfürstenstr. 76, ☎ 93820, IV-V ◉
Gh Pütz, Kurfürstenstr. 38, ☎ 5149, II ◉
Gh Sängerheim Rachtig, Gestadestr. 5, ☎ 3659, II
Gh Weinstube Moselblümchen, Fährstr. 18, ☎ 2403, II
Gh Weingut Kunz-Erben, Burgstr. 17, ☎ 4295
P Weingut Peter Ehses, Uferallee 49, ☎ 2838, II ◉
P Rebstock, Weingartenstr. 78, ☎ 2024, II

P Zum Himmelreich, Fährstr. 22, ✆ 2435, II

P Weinhof Morbach, Pastor-Glesiusstrasse 16, ✆ 3191, III

⛺ Campingplatz, Uferallee, ✆ 2404

Ürzig (L)
Postal code: 54539; Area code: 06532

H Alter Klosterhof, Würzgartenstr. 1, ✆ 2203, III-IV

H Zur Traube, Am Moselufer, ✆ 9308302, III-V

H Moselschild, Moselufer 14, ✆ 93930, V-VII

H Zehnthof, Moselufer 38, ✆ 2519, V

Hg Ürziger Ratskeller, Rathausplatz 10, ✆ 2260, IV

Erden (R)
Postal code: 54492; Area code: 06532

P Gästehaus u. Weingut Lotz, Hauptstr. 71, ✆ 3029, III

H Zum Moseltal, Am Moselufer 18, ✆ 2227, II-III

P Weingut Schwaab, Am Moselufer 5, ✆ 4711, II

P Weinhof St. Anna, Brückenstr. 2, ✆ 2354, II-III

P Franzen, Am Moselufer 9, ✆ 2032, II

Pz Gästehaus Marika, Fährstr. 2-4, ✆ 4624, II

⛺ Campingplatz, ✆ 4060

Lösnich (R)
Postal code: 54492; Area code: 06532

H Heil, Hauptstr. 15, ✆ 2223, III-V

H Zum Treppchen, Fischerg. 5, ✆ 93800, IV-V

P Kiebel, Hauptstr. 67-69, ✆ 2018

P Orthmann, Hauptstr. 29-31, ✆ 3266, II

P Simon, Untergasse 2, ✆ 2214

Kindel (R)
Postal code: 54538; Area code: 06532

ℹ Tourist-Information Kinheim, Moselweinstr. 14, ✆ 3444

H Im Winkel, Goldg. 5, ✆ 2584, III-IV

Pz Reschke, Brückenstr. 21, ✆ 4976, II-III

Pz Weingut Rieth, Brückenstr. 37, ✆ 2109, III 🔲

Kinheim (L)
Postal code: 54538; Area code: 06532

ℹ Tourist-Information Kinheim, Moselweinstr. 14, ✆ 3444

H Zum Rosenberg, Moselweinstr. 3, ✆ 2196, V

Gh Molitor, Kröver Str. 41, ✆ 2633, III

Kröv (L)
Postal code: 54536; Area code: 06541

ℹ Tourist-Information Kröv, Moselweinstr. 35, ✆ 9486

H Echternacher Hof, Moselweinstr. 24, ✆ 2438, III-IV

H Ratskeller, Robert-Schuman-Str. 49, ✆ 9997, III-V

H Reichsschenke Zum Ritter Götz, Robert-Schuman-Str. 57, ✆ 8166, IV-V

H Springiersbacher Hof, R.-Schumann-Str. 44, ✆ 1451, III-V

H Haus Sonnenlay, Im Flurgarten 19, ✆ 9660, IV

H Haus Mosella, Im Flurgarten 2, ✆ 9665, III-IV

H Moselterrasse, Moselweinstr. 27, ✆ 1521, IV

H Schäfer-Joisten, Robert-Schuman-Str. 78, ✆ 6337, III-IV

P Gutsweinschenke Müllers, Robert-Schuman-Str. 79 u. 59, ✆ 5365, III-V 🔲

P Weingut Knodt-Trossen, Plenterstr. 47, ✆ 4795

Pz Allmacher, Buchweg 10, ✆ 9793

⛺ Campingpl. Kröv, ✆ 06541/1669

Wolf (R)
Postal code: 56841; Area code: 06541

H Wolfshof, Klosterbergstr. 8, ✆ 860810, V

H Am Ufer, Uferstr. 5, ✆ 6993, V

P Haus Schatzgarten, Im Luxgraben 7, ✆ 9632, III

P Reinhard, Am Spielpl. 2, ✆ 9598, II

P Weingut Gass, Fährstr. 11, ✆ 1603, II 🔲

Pz Weingut Boor, Uferstr. 10, ✆ 6130, II

Pz Göhl, Baldesgraben 15, ✆ 6345, II

Pz Michels, Im Herrengarten 8, ✆ 9976, II

Pz Erbes, Im Spinnfeld 5, ✆ 6664, II

⛺ Campingpl. Wolf, Wedenhofstr. 25, ✆ 9174

Rißbach (L)
Postal code: 56841; Area code: 06541

⛺ Campingpl. Rißbach, Rißbacherstr. 165, ✆ 3111

Traben-Trarbach
Postal code: 56841; Area code: 06541

ℹ Tourist-Information, Am Bahnhof 5, ✆ 83980

🛏 Jugendherberge, Hirtenpfad 6, ✆ 9278 🔲

Traben (L)
H Zum Anker, Rißbacher Str. 3, ✆ 83080, IV-V

H Trabener Hof, Bahnstr. 25, ✆ 70080, V-VI 🔲

H Central-Hotel, Bahnstr. 43, ✆ 6238, IV-V

H Moselschlösschen, An der Mosel 14-15, ✆ 8320, VI-VII 🔲

H Bellevue, An der Mosel 11, ✆ 7030, VI-VII

H Bisenius, An der Mosel 56, ✆ 813710, V

H Vier Löwen, An der Mosel 12, ✆ 815908, V

H Krone, An der Mosel 93, ✆ 818668, V

P Cafe Balles, An der Mosel 20, ✆ 6944, III

P Trossen, Alter Brauer Weg 6, ✆ 2937, IV

P Clauß, Kirchstr. 7, ✆ 6347, II

P Pfeifer, Kräuterhausweg 19, ✆ 6065, III

P Kreischer, Kräuterhausweg 63, ✆ 9785, II-III 🔲

Pz Haus Würzgarten, Litziger Hirtenpfad 1, ✆ 1006, II-III

Pz Goebel, Kirchstr. 17, ✆ 9187, II

Trarbach (R)
P Altstadt-Café, Mittelstr. 12, ✆ 810625, III 🔲

H Gonzlay, Am Goldbach 3, ✆ 8360, V

H Zur goldenen Traube, Am Markt 8, ✆ 6011, IV-V

H Park-Hotel, Enkircher Str. 1-3, ✆ 811740, V

H Moseltor, Moselstr. 1, ✆ 6551, V-VI

Bad Wildstein (R)

Postal code: 56841; Area code: 06541

H Bad Wildstein, Bad Wildstein 2, ✆ 1001, IV

H Gräffs-Mühle, Wildbadstr. 217, ✆ 6331, IV-V ◉

H Haus Jungenwald, Wildbadstr. 227, ✆ 818491, V

P Bartz, Wildbadstr. 161, ✆ 9910, III

P Am Kurpark, Wildbadstr. 214, ✆ 819820, II-III

Kövenig (L)

Postal code: 54536; Area code: 06541

ℹ Tourist-Information Kröv, Moselweinstr. 35, ✆ 9486

P Gästehaus Doris, Moselstr. 26, ✆ 6310, II ◉

Enkirch (R)

Postal code: 56850; Area code: 06541

H Moselromantik-Hotel Dampfmühle, Am Steffensberg 80, ✆ 813950, V ◉

Pz Weingut Conrad Im Bungert 32, ✆ 9987, III

H Steffensberg, Brunnenpl. 1, ✆ 813960, IV-V

H Loosen, Bahnhofstr. 6+13, ✆ 6328, III-V

H Sponheimer Hof, Sponheimerstr. 19-23, ✆ 6628, III

H Gambrinus, Am Steffensberg 27, ✆ 4141, III

Gh Zum Weinstock, Weing. 5, ✆ 6237, II-III

Gh Zur Sonne, Sonnenstr. 1, ✆ 1565, II-III

Gh Alte Weinstube, Backhausstr. 4, ✆ 9335, II-III

P Schütz, Am Wallgraben 22, ✆ 9834, II

P Mohr, Backhausstr. 10, ✆ 814495, II

Pz Kettermann, Berliner Str. 11, ✆ 9764, II-III

Pz Spier-Immich, Königstr. 14a, ✆ 3363, II

Pz Demant, Am Steffensberg 17, ✆ 814651, II

Pz Bautz, Am Steffensberg 41, ✆ 9708, II-III

Pz Tempelhof, Tempelstr. 5, ✆ 6414, II

Pz Weisgerber, Am Steffensberg 66, ✆ 810081, II-III

Burg a. d. Mosel (R)

Postal code: 56843; Area code: 06541

H Zum Weinberg, Moselstr. 29, ✆ 9263, III

Gh Zur Post, Moselstr. 18, ✆ 9214, IV-V

P Haus Sylvia, Schlusstr. 16, ✆ 6763, II

P Falklay, Kirchstr. 8, ✆ 9270, II-III

P Weingut Heidhof, Schulstr. 27, ✆ 83940, III

Pz Bucher, Enkircher Weg 7, ✆ 6752, II

Pz Müller, In der Olk 1, ✆ 6982, II-III

Pz Conrad, In der Olk 4, ✆ 9260, II

Pz Heinz Conrad, Im Bungert 1, ✆ 6882, II ◉

Pz Weingut Meurer, In der Olk 15, ✆ 6766, II-III

Reil (L)

Postal code: 56861; Area code: 06542

ℹ Tourist-Information Reil, Hutg. 16, ✆ 21036

H Weinhaus Nalbach, Bergstr. 18, ✆ 2572, III-IV

H Reiler Hof, Moselweinstr. 27, ✆ 2629, III-V

H Zur Linde, Kaiser Str. 9, ✆ 2414, III-IV

H Weingut & Weinhaus Peter, Dorfstr. 17, ✆ 2415, III

P Haus Karina, Moselstr. 21, ✆ 21854, II-III ◉

P Haus Hedwig, Moselstr. 7, ✆ 22532, II ◉

P Weingut Müller, Küferstr. 15, ✆ 21467, II-III

Pünderich (R)

Postal code: 56862; Area code: 06542

H Weinhaus Lenz, Hauptstr. 31, ✆ 2350, III-V

H Alte Dorfschenke, Marienburgerstr. 20, ✆ 2897, II

Gh Weingut Lütz, Hauptstr. 50, ✆ 2769, III

P Mees, Hauptstr. 27, ✆ 21512, II

P Weingut Dahm, Bahnhofstr. 4, ✆ 2805

P Weingut Paulushof, Im Wingert 42, ✆ 22609, III

#Pz Busch, Springiersbacher Str. 33, ✆ 2551, II

Pz Franzen, Rathausstr. 15, ✆ 2907, II

Pz Ferienweingut Rockenbach, Hauptstr. 7, ✆ 2901, III

c Campingplatz Marienburg, Am Moselufer, ✆ 22009

c Campingplatz Moselland, Am Moselufer, ✆ 2618

Briedel (R)

Postal code: 56867; Area code: 06542

H Briedeler Haus, Hauptstr. 8, ✆ 4237, III

H Zum Musikalischen Wirt, Hauptstr. 97, ✆ 4589, III-IV

Gh Anker, Moselstr. 27, ✆ 5040, II-III

P Gibbert-Pohl, Moselstr. 4, ✆ 41270, III

Pz Schneiders-Reis, Gartenstr. 60, ✆ 4768, II

Pz Weingut Reis, Gartenstr. 43, ✆ 5711, II

Pz Weingut Goeres, Gartenstr. 36, ✆ 960091, II

Pz Feit, Hauptstr. 162, ✆ 41066, II

Pz Nalbach, Im Wallgraben 1, ✆ 4789, II

Zell (R)

Postal code: 56856; Area code: 06542

H Mayer, Balduinstr. 5-7, ✆ 61169, V-VI

H Zur Post, Schlossstr. 19-25, ✆ 4217, V ◉

H Ratskeller, Balduinstr. 36, ✆ 98620, V

H Zum Grünen Kranz, Balduinstr. 12, ✆ 98610, VI

Hg Café im Hamm, Merler Str. 5, ✆ 4566, IV

Hg Haus Notenau, Notenau 7-8, ✆ 5010, IV

P Grünewald, Heinzenberg 24, ✆ 4363, II-III

P Wein- und Sektgut Wagner, In Spay 1, ✆ 2998, II-III

P Weingut Scheid, Neue Kehr 1, ✆ 2337, III ◉

P Marientaler Au, Marientaler Au 30, ✆ 4261, III

P Bremm-Keltenhof, Kaimt, Kapellenstr. 1, ✆ 5420, III

P Schier, St. Johannis-Graben 1, ✆ 5434, II-III

P Haus Edeltraud, Kaimt, Kurtrierer Str. 33, ✆ 4628, III

P Reinisch, Balduinstr. 77, ✆ 4580, IV

P Gutsweinschänke Koch, Schlossstr. 10, ✆ 5227, IV ◉

⛺ Campingpark Zell/Mosel, Kaimt, ✆ 961216

Bullay (R)

Postal code: 56859; Area code: 06542

H Moselperle, Königswiese 4, ✆ 93640, IV-V
Gh Spies, Kirchstr. 35, ✆ 2541, II
Gh Café Görgen, Bahnhofstr. 32, ✆ 2519, III
P Wagner, Bahnhofstr. 18, ✆ 2586, III
P Budinger, Lindenpl. 6, ✆ 2355, II-III
P Moselinchen, Graf-Beisel-Str. 6, ✆ 900664, II-III
P Gästehaus Münster, Moselstr. 7, ✆ 2383, II 📶
Pz Eberhard, Alte Poststr. 15, ✆ 22684, II
Pz Gippert, Alte Poststr. 19, ✆ 2590, II
Pz Hehn und Roth, Zehthausstr. 14+16, ✆ 21650, III
Pz Wirtz, Brautrockstr. 10, ✆ 22819, I-II
🏕 Bären-Camp, Am Moselufer 1, ✆ 900097 📶
🏕 Campingplatz Moselblick, Am Moselufer 2, ✆ 900024

Alf (L)

Postal code: 56859; Area code: 06542

H Flairhotel Bömers Mosellandhotel, Ferdinand-Re-my-Str. 27, ✆ 2310, V 📶
H Burg Arras, ✆ 22275, VI-VII
H Bellevue Mosel-Hotel Alf, Am Moselufer, Mosel-str. 1, ✆ 2581, III-V 📶
Hg Herrenberg, Moselstr. 11, ✆ 2638, III
P Haus Budinger, Brückenstr. 7, ✆ 2671, II
Pz Bauer-Thiel, Mühlenstr. 45, ✆ 1212, II-III

Pz Justen, Mühlenstr. 41, ✆ 21682, II

St. Aldegund (L)

Postal code: 56858; Area code: 06542

P Mosella, Am Moselstausee 41, ✆ 21703, III
P St. Aldegundishof, Am Moselstausee 39, ✆ 2575, III
P Schönblick, Klosterkammerstr. 59, ✆ 21257, II-III
Pz Krämer-Feiden, Am Moselstausee 38, ✆ 21635, II
Pz Scheid, Klosterkammerstr. 70, ✆ 1667, II-III

Neef (R)

Postal code: 56858; Area code: 06542

P Weingut Bremm, Moseluferstr. 16, ✆ 02675/910223, II-III
P Amlinger & Sohn, Moseluferstr. 17, ✆ 2962, III
P Haus Markert, Fährstr. 4, ✆ 2829, I-II
P Franzen, Petersbergstr. 67a, ✆ 22159, I
Pz Weingut Zecherhof, Auf der Kehr 20, ✆ 21717, III
Pz Bergen, Klosterstubenstr. 41, ✆ 21515, II
Pz Boendgen, Petersbergstr.1, ✆ 2872, II
Pz Weingut Nelius-Kirch, Bachtalstr. 30, ✆ 2637, I

Bremm (L)

Postal code: 56814; Area code: 02675

H Hutter, Moselstr. 30, ✆ 212, III
H Weinhaus Berg, Moselstr. 39, ✆ 301, III-IV 📶
Gh Pellenz, Moselstr. 32, ✆ 571, II-II
P Treis, Calmontstr. 16, ✆ 401, III
P Clemens, Auf Cales 22, ✆ 1262, II

Pz Franzen, Gartenstr. 52, ✆ 550, II

Ediger-Eller (L)

Postal code: 56814; Area code: 02675

H Moselromantik zum Löwen, Moselweinstr. 23, ✆ 208, IV-V
H Friderichs, Moselweinstr. 81, ✆ 237, II-III
H Römerstube, Moselweinstr. 9, ✆ 424, III-V
Pz Zenz, Hochstr. 29, ✆ 384, II

Ediger (L)

H Feiden, Moselweinstr. 22, ✆ 259, V
H Weinhaus St. Georg, Moselweinstr. 10, ✆ 205, III-V

Eller (L)

H Moselterrasse, Moselweinstr. 59, ✆ 278, IV
H Weinhaus Oster, Moselweinstr. 61-63, ✆ 232, III-V
P Gästehaus am Calmont, Moselweinstr. 83, ✆ 1356, III
🏕 Campingplatz z. Feuerberg, Stangenhahnstr. 6, ✆ 701

Nehren (L)

Postal code: 56820; Area code: 02673

P Quartier Andre, Moselstr. 1, ✆ 4015, III
P Rügner, Moselweinstr. 9, ✆ 962170
P Zur Pilsstube, Kirchstr. 10, ✆ 962439, II
P Weingut Holzknecht, Römerstr. 9a, ✆ 4282, II
P Liebfried, Moselstr. 13, ✆ 4290, II
🏕 Campingplatz Nehren, ✆ 4612

Senheim/Senhals

Postal code: 56820; Area code: 02673

ℹ Tourist Information Keltisches Weintal, Mosel-weinstr. 19, ✆ 960111
H Schützen, Brunnenstr. 13, ✆ 4306, III-IV 📶
P Ferienpension-Cafe Stenze, Neustr. 15, ✆ 4457, II
H Deis, Moselweinstr. 38, ✆ 4651, IV-V
H Weinhaus Halfenstube, Moselweinstr. 30, ✆ 4579, IV-V 📶
P Thiesen, Altmai 41, ✆ 4308, II
P Elvira, Am Gestade 8, ✆ 4479, III
P Moselblick, Fährstr. 17, ✆ 4458, II
Pz Weingut Karl Desoye, Brunnenstr. 15, ✆ 902406
🏕 Campingplatz Senheim, ✆ 4660

Mesenich (R)

Postal code: 56820; Area code: 02673

P Wein und Gästehaus M. Bai, Zehnthofstr. 11, ✆ 4558, IV
H Andries, Am Bühl 7, ✆ 4578, III
Gh Freimuth, Wiesenweg 19, ✆ 4385, II
P Schneiders-Andres, Briederner Weg 29, ✆ 4295, II
P Servaty's Sonnhof, Wiesenweg 29, ✆ 4020, II-III
Pz Weingut Arens Hirschen, Pützstr. 12, ✆ 4529, II
Pz Pauly, Briederner Weg 15, ✆ 4573, II
Pz Kochems, Wiesenweg 31, ✆ 4524, II
Pz Andres, Briederner Weg 8, ✆ 4301, II

145

Family Camping Club, Wiesenweg 25, ✆ 4556

Briedern (R)
Postal code: 56820; Area code: 02673
H Zum Moselstrand, Moselstr. 20, ✆ 1748, III-IV
Gh Rebstock, Moselstr. 24, ✆ 1633, III
Gh Brodam, Im Hofgraben 12, ✆ 1856, II
Gh Mönch, Moselstr. 3, ✆ 1835, II
P Lenz, Moselstr. 11, ✆ 1659, III-IV
P Weingut Friedrich, Römerstr. 37, ✆ 1300, II-III
Pz Arnoldi, Wiesengrund 1, ✆ 1479, II
Pz Lenartz-Bleser, Hauptstr. 20, ✆ 1442, II
Pz Scheuren, Römerstr. 11, ✆ 1477, II

Beilstein (R)
Postal code: 56814; Area code: 02673
Verkehrsverein, Bachstr. 47, ✆ 900191
H Altes Zollhaus und Am Klosterberg, Auf dem Teich 8, ✆ 1850, IV-V
H Burgfrieden, Im Mühlental 17, ✆ 93639, IV-V
H Haus Burg Metternich, Moselstr. 1-2, ✆ 1756, III-IV
H Haus Lipmann, Marktpl. 3, ✆ 1573, V
H Gute Quelle, Marktpl. 34, ✆ 1437, III-IV
P Haus Erika, Kurierweg 9, ✆ 1449, II-III
P Jobelius, Auf dem Teich 4, ✆ 1583, II
P Haus Johanna, Alte Wehrstr. 23, ✆ 1483, II-III

Ellenz-Poltersdorf (L)
Postal code: 56821; Area code: 02673

H Ellenzer Goldbäumchen, Moselweinstr. 17, ✆ 1416, III-IV
H Fuhrmann, Moselweinstr. 21, ✆ 9310, III-V
H Vergißmeinnicht, Weinstr. 20, ✆ 1721, IV
H Dehren, Kurfürstenstr. 30, ✆ 1325, IV-V
H Alte Weinschänke, Kurfürstenstr. 35, ✆ 1421, III
Gh Könen, Moselweinstr. 8, ✆ 1883, II-III
P Steinfelder Hof, Hauptstr. 21, ✆ 1879, III-IV
P Ferienweingut Schneider, Am Stausee 2, ✆ 1581, II
Pz Fuhrmann, Hauptstr. 17, ✆ 1394, II
Pz Fett, Goldbäumchenstr. 26, ✆ 1465, II
Pz Clemens, Weinstr. 8, ✆ 1387, III
Pz Könen-Klaus, Goldbäumchenstr. 5, ✆ 1673, II
Pz Boos, Hauptstr. 75, ✆ 1867, II
Pz Fuhrmann, Auf der Burg 9, ✆ 1372, II
Pz Portugall, Im Bernert 8, ✆ 1537, II
Pz Schausten-Feldhausen, Kurfürstenstr. 15, ✆ 1348, II
Pz Hermes, St. Sebastianusstr. 9, ✆ 1845, II
Campingplatz, Moselweinstraße, ✆ 1272

Bruttig (R)
Postal code: 56814; Area code: 02671
H Mosellanus, Hauptstr. 19, ✆ 7138, III
H Zum guten Onkel, Bergstr. 6, ✆ 7141, IV-V
P Alte Winzerschenke, Am Moselufer 7, ✆ 989047, II

P Haus Mühlenruh, Mühlenbachstr. 26, ✆ 7931, II
P Hirschen, Petrus-Mosellanus-Str. 1, ✆ 4508, II-III
P Panorama, Tannenweg 12, ✆ 4175, II
Pz Andrae, Gartenstr. 2, ✆ 1475, II
Campingplatz Bruttig, Am Moselufer, ✆ 915429

Fankel (R)
Postal code: 56814; Area code: 02671
P Brunnenhof, Brunnenstr. 32, ✆ 7713, II-III
P Laux, Moselstr. 1, ✆ 8128, II-III
Gh Weingut Riedel Hauptstr. 34, ✆ 4705
Gh Steuer, Erlenweg 2, ✆ 3527, II
Gh Schmiedel, Ahornweg 15, ✆ 4785, II
Pz Weingut Hess-Becker, Christophorusweg 8, ✆ 8117, III-IV

Ernst (L)
Postal code: 56814; Area code: 02671
H Pollmanns, Moselstr. 53-55, ✆ 8683, V
H Filla Andre, Moselstr. 1, ✆ 4688, III-IV
H Traube, Moselstr. 33, ✆ 980205, III
H Zur Winzergenossenschaft, Moselstr. 59, ✆ 7091, III
Gh Kirch, Herrenstr. 16, ✆ 4495
P Haus Sonnenschein, Klosterstr. 12, ✆ 7444, IV
P Konschake, Auf der Winneburg 15, ✆ 7452, II-IV
P Weingarten, Moselweinstr. 9, ✆ 1404, IV
Pz Haus Barden, Moselstr. 37, ✆ 7799, II

Pz Junglas, Herrenstr. 13, ✆ 8753, II
Pz Zenz, Moselstr. 44, ✆ 7345, III
Pz Gansen, Weingartenstr. 29, ✆ 1518, II
Pz Göbel-Schausten, Moselstr. 36, ✆ 3132, II-III

Valwig (R)
Postal code: 56812; Area code: 02671
Tourist-Information, Sonnenhang 10, ✆ 9150284
Gh Altes Winzerhaus, Bachstr. 4, ✆ 7330, II-III
H Fritz, Moselweinstr. 60, ✆ 7475, III-IV
Gh Beim Schneemann, Brühlstr. 2, ✆ 3116, III-IV
Gh Andries, Moselweinstr. 11, ✆ 8696, II-III
P Beth-Steuer, Brühlstr. 9, ✆ 7358, III-IV
P Haus Mosella, Moselweinstr. 10, ✆ 7313, II-III

Cochem
Postal code: 56812; Area code: 02671
Tourist-Information Ferienland Cochem, Endertpl. 1, ✆ 60040
Gh Zum Fröhlichen Weinberg, Schlaufstr. 11, ✆ 4193, II
H Am Hafen, Uferstr. 3, ✆ 97720, V-VI
H Germania, Moselpromenade 1, ✆ 97750, V-VI
H Moselromantik, Am Reilsbach 12, ✆ 4600, V
H Müller, Moselpromenade 9, ✆ 1333, V
H Panorama, Klostergartenstr. 42-44, ✆ 914140, V-VI
H Parkhotel, Sehler Anlagen 1, ✆ 7110, V-VI
H Thul, Brauselaystr. 27, ✆ 914150, V-VI

H Zur Weinhexe, Hafenstr. 1, ✆ 97760, V

H Zur Schönen Aussicht, Sehler Anlagen 22, ✆ 7232, V

H Weinhof, Moselpromenade 27, ✆ 7462, III-V 📷

H Moselflair, Bergstr. 6, ✆ 8894, V-VI 📷

Hg Am Rosenhügel, Valwiger Str. 57, ✆ 97630, V-VI

Hg Friedrichs, Endertstr. 138, ✆ 7467, III-IV

Gh Onkel Willi, Endertstr. 39, ✆ 7305, V

Gh Zum edlen Tropfen, Talstraße, ✆ 4168, III

P Hendriks, Jahnstr. 8, ✆ 917361, II-V

P Dohler, Valwigerstr. 41, ✆ 7696, II-III

P Villa Tummelchen, Schlossstr. 22, ✆ 910520, V-VI 📷

P Elisabeth, Zehnthausstr. 52-54, ✆ 5201, II-IV

P Regina, Remaclusstr. 2, ✆ 7262, III-V

P Lange, Endertstr. 52, ✆ 7173, II-III

Pz Weingut Rademacher, Pinner Str. 10, ✆ 4164, II-III

Pz Haus Rossi, Zehnthausstr. 65, ✆ 1503, II-III

Pz Winzerhof, Endertstr. 24-28, ✆ 7297, II-III

Pz Michels, In der Märtschelt 12/14, ✆ 3395, II-III

Pz Bach, Im Brühl 30, ✆ 3151, II-III

Pz Bamberg, Schlossstr. 5, ✆ 7056, II

Pz Bremm, Remaclusstr. 1, ✆ 91281, III

Pz Altes Fährhaus, Uferstr. 19, ✆ 605527, II-III

Pz Höhn, Schubertstr. 27, ✆ 1656, II-III

Pz Ostermann, Kaasstr. 11, ✆ 1601, II-III

Pz Sigismund, Maria-Hell-Str. 4, ✆ 4436, II

Pz Thiel, Zehnthausstr. 13, ✆ 4239, II-III

Pz Wagner, Schubertstr. 23, ✆ 3315, II

🏠 Moseltal-Jugendherberge, Klottener Str. 9, ✆ 8633 📷

🅰 Am Freizeitentrum, Moritzburger Str. 1, ✆ 4409

🅰 Schausten-Reif, Endertstr. 124, ✆ 7528

🅰 Zur Winneburg, Endertstr. 141, ✆ 98730

Klotten (L)

Postal code: 56818; Area code: 02671

H Hubertus, Hauptstr. 35, ✆ 7391, IV-V

H Zur Post, Bahnhofstr. 24, ✆ 7116, V 📷

H Weingut Kapellenhof, Am Kapellenberg 14, ✆ 1261, IV

H Zur Linde, Moselstr. 19, ✆ 4376, III

Pz Haus Agnes, Im Weingarten 16, ✆ 7380, II

Pz Loosen, Mittelstr. 12, ✆ 7501, II

Pz Michels, Bahnhofstr. 22, ✆ 1251, II

Pz Bertram, Untere-Brühlstr. 5A, ✆ 1366, II 📷

Pommern (L)

Postal code: 56829; Area code: 02672

🛈 Tourist-Info Treis-Karden, St.-Castor-Str. 87, ✆ 9157700

Gh Onkel Otto, Lindenstr. 13, ✆ 2407, III 📷

Gh Hermes, Hauptstr. 14, ✆ 7010, II

Gh Henerichs, Hauptstr. 43, ✆ 2536, II-III

P Weinhaus Schneiders, Moselweinstr. 5, ✆ 2159, II

Pz Weingut Schneiders, Bahnhofstr. 2, ✆ 2531, II

Pz Hammes, Im Bachtal 2, ✆ 1754, II

Pz Schneiders, Zehnthofstr. 24, ✆ 2085, II

Pz Weingut Zenzen, Bahnhofstr. 7, ✆ 2520, II

🅰 Campingplatz Pommern, Moselweinstraße, ✆ 2461

Treis-Karden

Postal code: 56253; Area code: 02672

🛈 Tourist-Info, St.-Castor-Str. 87, ✆ 9157700

Treis (R)

H Moselblick, Moselallee 13-14 ✆ 7197, III-IV 📷

H Ostermann, Lützbach, ✆ 1238, IV-V

Gh Gräf, Lisbergstr. 2, ✆ 7227, II

Gh Rathausschänke, Hauptstr. 32, ✆ 1210, II-III

Gh Bike-Inn, Brückenstr. 17, ✆ 913558, III

Gh Brückenschänke, Brückenstr. 16, ✆ 2409, III

P Weingut Knaup, Am Rathaus 6, ✆ 2446, II

Pz Haus Reis, Moselallee 23, ✆ 1298, III 📷

Pz Haus Born-Simon, Kirchberger Str. 9, ✆ 1413, II

Pz Fuhrmann, Forststr. 52, ✆ 7395, II

Pz Löhr, Kastellauner Straße, ✆ 910118, II

Pz Neef, Auf der Hohl 12, ✆ 7534, II

Pz Seibold, Fischerg. 13, ✆ 1349, II

Karden (L)

H Schlosshotel Petry, St. Castor Str. 80, ✆ 9340, V-VI

H Am Stiftstor, St. Castor-Str. 17, ✆ 1363, IV

H Brauer, Moselstr. 25-26, ✆ 1211, IV

Gh Zur Linde, St. Castor-Str. 10, ✆ 1360, III

P Zimmer-Frei-Burg Eltz, Burg-Eltz-Weg 2, ✆ 913666, III

Pz Ferienhaus Barz, St. Castor-Str. 60, ✆ 2996, II

Hh Klickerterhof, Klickerterhof, ✆ 7156, II

🅰 Campingplatz Mosel-Boating-Center, ✆ 2613

Müden (L)

Postal code: 56254; Area code: 02672

🛈 Tourist-Info Treis-Karden, St.-Castor-Str. 87, ✆ 9157700

H Sewenig, Moselstr. 5, ✆ 1334, V

H Sonnenhof, Silberstr. 33, ✆ 7463, III

Gh Balthasar, Hauptstr. 16, ✆ 910166, III

P Weingut Dehen, Görresstr. 7, ✆ 1309, II

P Zur Linde, Fährstr. 10, ✆ 7987, II

Moselkern (L)

Postal code: 56254; Area code: 02672

🛈 Tourist-Info Treis-Karden, St.-Castor-Str., ✆ 9157700

Pz Pauly, Oberstr. 53, ✆ 7085, II 📷

H Ringelsteiner Mühle, Elztal 95, ✆ 910200, V

H Moselkern, Moselstr. 15, ✆ 1303, IV

P Zur Burg Eltz, Oberstr. 54, ✆ 2731, III

Pz Grolig, Elztal 27, ✆ 1567, II 📷

Pz Henrich, Oberstr. 49, ✆ 2554, II

Pz Kalmes, Oberstr. 56, ✆ 1668, II 📶

🏕 Campingplatz zur Burg Eltz, Moselstr. 39, ✆ 9135861

Burgen (R)
Postal code: 56332; Area code: 02605

H Schmause-Mühle, Baybachstr. 50, ✆ 776, III-IV

H Forellenzucht, Baybachtal, ✆ 4640, III-IV

P Haus Bischofstein, Moselstr. 16, ✆ 4558, II

🏕 Campingplatz Laguna, An der Mosel, ✆ 952176

🏕 Campingplatz Burgen, An der Mosel, ✆ 2396

Wierschem (L)
Postal code: 56294; Area code: 02605

H Landhaus Neuhof, Burg Eltz Str. 23, ✆ 565, II-III

Münstermaifeld (L)
Postal code: 56294; Area code: 02605

H Athen, Obertorstr. 4-6, ✆ 1715, V

Gh Deutsches Haus, Untertorstr. 24, ✆ 704, II

Hatzenport (L)
Postal code: 56332; Area code: 02605

Gh Zur Traube, Moselstr. 10, ✆ 777, II-III 📶

H Rosenhof, Oberstr. 74, ✆ 962713, III

H Winzerhof Gietzen, Moselstr. 70, ✆ 952371, III-IV 📶

H Weinhaus Ibald, Moselstr. 34, ✆ 2043, III 📶

Gh Brunnenhof Winzer Bernard Ibald, Moselstr. 58,

✆ 952485, II-III 📶

P Bröhl, Moselstr. 62, ✆ 2605, III

Brodenbach (R)
Postal code:56332; Area code: 02605

H Anker, Moselufer 15, ✆ 2008, III-V

H Peifer, Moselstr. 43, ✆ 756, III-V

H Dähler Stuben, Ehrenburgertal 30, ✆ 3022, V

P Elisabeth, Moselufer 30, ✆ 2456, II

P Haus Christiane, Salzwiese 27, ✆ 2388, II

P Haus am Walde, Salzwiese 16, ✆ 2331, II

P Konditorei Café Welling, Rhein-Mosel-Str. 37, ✆ 642, II-III

🏕 Vogelsang, Rhein-Mosel-Str. 63, ✆ 1437

Löf (L)
Postal code: 56332; Area code: 02605

H Lellmann, Alte Moselstr. 36, ✆ 98070, IV-V

H Krähennest, Moselstern Hotels, Auf der Kräh 2, ✆ 8080, V-VII

H Zur Traube, Alte Moselstr. 2, ✆ 98080, IV-V

Gh Café Braun, Alte Moselstr. 51, ✆ 3315, II-III 📶

P Haus Luzia, Bahnhofstr. 7, ✆ 2189, II

Alken (R)
Postal code: 56332; Area code: 02605

H Landhaus Müller, Moselstr. 6, ✆ 952512, IV-V

H Landhaus Schnee, Moselstr. 1, ✆ 3383, IV-V

H Winzerhof Brachtendorf, Maltheserstr. 4-6,

✆ 2805, III

H Moselhotel Burg Café, Moselstr. 11, ✆ 4443, IV-V

Hg Café Becker, Von-Wiltberg-Str. 1, ✆ 96320, III-IV

Gh Burg Thurant, Moselstr. 15, ✆ 3581, IV

Gh Moselblick, Moselstr. 12, ✆ 3347, III-IV

P Becker, Von-Wiltberg-Str. 1, ✆ 96320, III

Pz Haus Inge, Mittelstr. 28, ✆ 3106, II

Pz Haus Walburga, Mittelstr. 3, ✆ 590, II

Kattenes (L)
Postal code: 56332; Area code: 02605

H Langen, Oberdorfstr. 6, ✆ 4575, III 📶

P Panorama, Panoramastr. 1, ✆ 960137, III

P Weingut Gästezimmer Gutsschank Fries, Moselufer 14, ✆ 2001, III

Pz Erika, Panoramastr. 8a, ✆ 3917, I-II

Pz Weingut Leyendecker, Moselufer 13, ✆ 84649, III

Oberfell (R)
Postal code: 56332; Area code: 02605

Gh Zur Krone, Moselstr. 11, ✆ 665, III

Gh Schweisthal, Moselstr. 21, ✆ 604, III

P Birkenhof, Hauptstr. 52, ✆ 8830, IV

Niederfell (R)
Postal code: 56332; Area code: 02607

H Restaurant Kastanienhof, Moselstr. 47, ✆ 8680, IV

Gh Zur Mühle, Bachstr. 33, ✆ 6505, II-III

Gh Traube, Moselstr. 27, ✆ 249, III-IV

P Café Sander, Moselstr. 15, ✆ 8309, III-IV

P Ulla, Bergstr. 20, ✆ 2085, III-V

P Haus Andries, Lennigstr. 17, 6164, II-III

Pz Weingut Künster, Moselstr. 19, ✆ 6524, II

Pz Haus Lorscheid, Marktstr. 61, ✆ 312, I-II

Kobern-Gondorf (L)
Postal code: 56330; Area code: 02607

ℹ Touristbüro, Kirchstr. 1, ✆ 1055

Gh Zur Kupferkanne, Lutzstr. 20, ✆ 342, IV-V 📶

H Simonis, Marktpl. 4, ✆ 203, V

Hg Weinhaus Moselschänke, Marktpl. 20, ✆ 384, III 📶

Gh Kastorschänke, Fährstr. 20, ✆ 972037, III-V 📶

P Marienhof, Römerstr. 7, ✆ 4593, III

Pz Haus Vogt, Münsterberg 10, ✆ 4114, II-IV 📶

Pz Haus Löhr, Lubentiusstr. 5, ✆ 4736, II-III

Pz Landhaus Julia, Im Geispfad 13, ✆ 1895, II-III 📶

Fw Im alten Hof, Maifeldstr. 10, ✆ 972086 📶

Dieblich (R)
Postal code: 56332; Area code: 02607

H Pistono, Hauptstr. 30, ✆ 218, III-V

H Burghof, Fährstr. 19, ✆ 6066, III-IV

H Kachelburg, Kegelbahnstr. 15, ✆ 940555, IV

Gh Moselgruß, Hauptstr. 56, ✆ 223, III

Winningen (L)
Postal code: 56333; Area code: 02606

🄳 Touristik Winningen, Aug.-Horch-Str. 3, ☎ 2214

P Haus Edith, Zehnhofstr. 9, ☎ 2204, II

H Moselblick, An der B 416, ☎ 920810, V

H Adler, Fronstr. 10, ☎ 806, III

H Nora Emmerich, Raiffeisenstr. 15, ☎ 537, IV

Gh Zum Fährhof, Fährstr. 16, ☎ 92010, IV 🄼

P Horch, Fährstr. 19, ☎ 2284, III

P Weinhaus Marktschenke, Am Markt 5, ☎ 355, IV

Pz Gästehaus Mäder, Raiffeisenstr. 12, ☎ 1688, IV-V

Pz Weingut Hess-Hautt, Aug.-Horch-Str 20, ☎ 438, II

Pz Haus Sturm, In der Ach 41, ☎ 2335, II

🄰 Insel Ziehfurt, Fährstr. 35, ☎ 1800

Koblenz
Postal code: 56068; Area code: 0261

🄳 Koblenz-Touristik, Bahnhofpl. 7, ☎ 303880

H Hamm, St. Josef-Str. 32-34, ☎ 303210, V

H Kornpforte, Kornpfortstr. 11, ☎ 31174, IV-V

H Ibis Koblenz, Rizzastr. 42, ☎ 30240, V

H Mercure, Julius-Wegeler-Str. 6, ☎ 1360, VI

H Brenner, Rizzastr. 20-22, ☎ 915780, IV-V

H Hohenstaufen, Emil-Schüller-Str. 41-43, ☎ 30140, V 🄼

H Jan van Werth, Von-Werth-Str. 9, ☎ 36500, IV

H Trierer Hof, Clemensstr. 1, ☎ 10060, V

Hg Reinhard, Bahnhofstr. 60, ☎ 34835, III

Hg Cityhotel Kurfürst Balduin, Hohenfelderstr. 12, ☎ 13320, V-VI

🄰 Rhein-Mosel, 56070, Schartwiesenweg 6, ☎ 82719

Asterstein
Postal code: 56077; Area code: 0261

H Rheinkrone, Rudolf-Breitscheid-Str. 23, ☎ 9730803, IV-V

Ehrenbreitstein
Postal code: 56077; Area code: 0261

H Diehl's, Rheinsteigufer 1, ☎ 97070, V-VI 🄼

🄸 Koblenz, Festung Ehrenbreitstein, ☎ 972870

Güls
Postal code: 56072; Area code: 0261

H Weinhaus Grebel, Planstr. 7-9, ☎ 42530, V 🄼

H Gülser Weinstube, Moselweinstr. 3, ☎ 9886410, V

H Weinhaus Kreuter, Stauseestr. 31, ☎ 941470, IV-V 🄼

H Hähn, Wolfskaulstr. 94, ☎ 947230, III-IV

Gh Zum Rebstock, Poppenstr. 7, ☎ 42633, III-IV 🄼

P Haus Ursula, Steinebirker Weg 2, ☎ 44676 🄼

🄰 Gülser Moselbogen, Am Gülser Moselbogen 20, ☎ 44474

Lay
Postal code: 56073; Area code: 02606

H Anker, Maistr. 2, ☎ 2234, III-V

Lützel
Postal code: 56070; Area code: 0261

H Stein-Schiller´s Restaurant, Mayener Str. 126, ☎ 963530, VI 🄼

🄰 Rhein-Mosel, Schartwiesenweg 6, ☎ 82719

Metternich
Postal code: 56072; Area code: 0261

H Fährhaus am Stausee, An der Fähre 3, ☎ 927290, V 🄼

Moselweiß
Postal code: 56073; Area code: 0261

H Haus Bastian, Maigesetzweg 12, ☎ 922200, V

H Zum Schwarzen Bären, Koblenzer Str. 35, ☎ 4602700, IV-V 🄼

Neuendorf
Postal code: 56070; Area code: 0261

H Zum Hafen, Neuendorfer Str. 17, ☎ 9837852, III

Gh Alt Neuendorf, Am Ufer 23, ☎ 82847, IV 🄼

Pfaffendorf
Postal code: 56076; Area code: 0261

H Merkelbach, Emser Str. 87, ☎ 974410, V 🄼

Rauental
Postal code: 56073; Area code: 0261

H Contel, Pastor-Klein-Str. 19, ☎ 40650, V

H Scholz, Moselweißer Str. 121, ☎ 94260, V

H Hotel am Büropark Moselstausee, Schlachthof- str. 50, ☎ 408017, II-III 🄼

Thanks

Thanks to all those who helped us with the production of this guide. We especially wish to thank the following people for their helpful information: U. Schwaiger, Ravensburg; O. Brand, Frankfurt/Main; E., P. u. Th. Breitenberger, Kempten; G., E. u. M. Franitzer, Kempten; R., G. u. P. Ehlers, Kempten; K. Schäuble, Balingen; St. u. Th. Körber, Berlin; H. u. W. Neumann, Büttelborn; G. Göpel, Münzenberg; E. Wormstädt, Stuttgart; St. Decker, Bremen; S. Streck, Köln; R. Berniol, Stuttgart; H.-J. Dombrowsky, Nassau/Lahn; E. Wittmann, Weilheim; I. Hanschke, Friedrichsdorf; G. u. G. Lambrecht, Elchingen; M. Kramer u. C. Müller, Unadigen; R. u. R. Schlatter-Romann, Opfikon; H. Schilling; K. Jahre, Gelsenkirchen; M. Schneider, Stuttgart; H. Deters, Osnabrück; I. Hoferichter, Ibbenbüren; K. Sohn; W. Groove, Haan; L. Köhler, Lörrach; J. Laub u. B. Kadela, Markgröningen; S. Merz, Waldshut-Tiengen; W. Müller, Burg a. d. Mosel; D. Demmer, Mainz; B. Halter, Kobern-Gondorf; H. Haible, Sachsenheim; Dr. U. Wörtz, Waiblingen-Neustadt; K. Koch, Bitz; S. Waldmann, Wilhelmsdorf; K. Mander, Detzem; D. Kämpf, Stuttgart; E. Sartorius; D. Krüger, Wermelskirchen; Dr. H. Miska, Klein-Winternheim; E. Botsch; M. Volleth; T. Nies; P. u. M. Stahl, Kelsterbach; W. Schmetz; R. Wirsching; W. Buddelmann; U. Majewski; L. Browers; E.-M. Muelenz; E. Scheid; G. Kaminski; A. Wuensche; Fam. Höfle, Uhlingen; B. Gerlich, Nürnberg; U. Ambos; Dr. H. Schmidt, Bamberg; J. Reitgassl; C. Ganzhorn, Sindelfingen; E. Leuchert, Drensteinfurt; R. Körfer, Gladenbach; M.W. Reus, Bovenkarspel (NL); M. Rapp; H. Bergmann; E. Gerowski; J. Brunner; H. u. R. E. Böhm, Kaarst; Dr. H. Brunotte, Düsseldorf; W. Ebel; R. u. B. Westphal; H. Henneberg;E. Rüfenacht, Dulliken (CH); H. Eilinghoff; F. Mombrei, Hattersheim; B. Konold, Giengen/Brenz; B. Frey; Dr. H. Weisel, Ebermannstadt; Dr. W. Patzelt, Wetzlar; S. Weiß; R. Waldkönig, Konz; E. Lienau, Osnabrück; G. Oster, Schömberg; B. Brömel, Berlin; D. Birnbaum, Darmstadt; W. Pankewitz; M. Härdle; R. Wirsching; M. Kasparek; M. Ehses; Ch. Dillinger; K. Förster; W. König, Konz; S. Stolte; K. Werner; C. Liebers; H. Bischoff, Recklinghausen; C. Wallenwein; U. Eisel; E. Wohlenberg, Hamburg; A. Poth; K. u. R. Schröder; A. Wellmann, Leopoldshöhe; H. Ahrens; U. Meyer, Lübeck; D. u. A. Lindner; C. Dusi, Stans; D. Thesen; E. Oosterhof; K. Dreher, Salem; U. Schwabenland-Wurm; W. Bitzer; M. Schulte-Lünzum, Staufenberg; U. u. C. Pfeiffer, Bremen; T. Wild, Bergisch Gladbach; H. Loser, Jona; J. Enting; M. u. W. Dehoust, Schriesheim; A. Miehlke, Wilhelmshaven; P. Hoppe; C. Schmitz; G. Böhne, Heidelberg; L. Doerr; N. Meyer, Einhausen; E. Buttelmann; H.-G. Gonsior; M. Jung; C. Weiland, Freiburg; M. Weinhold; J. Wöstenfeld Aeschbacher; H. Kasulke, Bovenden; J. Howald, Zürich (CH); Dr. M. Dietrich; H. Walter, Hamburg; P. Schütz, Poprad (SK); U. True, Heemsen; H. u. R. Pietsch, Eppstein; I. Kühlke; S. Gleißner, Alf; J. Schaller, Winterthur (CH); H. Schüßler; M. Rist; H. Stelter; G. Kaes; M. Borgs; H. Reck; R. u. F. Kaminski; F. Voltenauer; M. Meffert, Lauterbach; A. u. M. Johanns, Krefeld; M. Doss

Geographical index

Page numbers in *green* refer to the overnight accommodation list.